SOLUTIONS FOR PROMOTING PRINCIPAL–TEACHER TRUST

Phyllis A. Gimbel

A SCARECROWEDUCATION BOOK

The Scarecrow Press, Inc.
Lanham, Maryland • Toronto • Oxford
2003

A SCARECROWEDUCATION BOOK

Published in the United States of America
by ScarecrowEducation
An imprint of The Rowman & Littlefield Publishing Group, Inc.
4501 Forbes Boulevard, Suite 200, Lanham, Maryland 20706
www.scarecroweducation.com

PO Box 317
Oxford
OX2 9RU, UK

British Library Cataloguing in Publication Information Available

Library of Congress Cataloging-in-Publication Data
Gimbel, Phyllis A., 1946–
    Solutions for promoting principal–teacher trust / Phyllis A. Gimbel.
      p. cm.
    "A ScarecrowEducation book."
    Includes bibliographical references and index.
    ISBN 1-57886-021-0 (pbk. : alk. paper)
  1. School principals—Psychology. 2. Teacher–principal relationships.
3. School environment. 4. Trust. I. Title.
LB2831.9.G56 2003
371.1'06—dc21   2003008246

∞™ The paper used in this publication meets the minimum requirements of
American National Standard for Information Sciences—Permanence of
Paper for Printed Library Materials, ANSI/NISO Z39.48-1992.
Manufactured in the United States of America.

For those who believed in me, precisely in this order: Belle Brunell, Rosemarie Cuomo, Dr. Emilie Stadler, Dr. Donald Oliver, Dr. Kevin Thomas Plodzik, Dr. John D. MacLean Jr., Dr. Sally L. Dias, and Dr. Annette Stavros.

CONTENTS

FOREWORD

There are ninety-two thousand principals in the United States. Half will retire within the next few years. How we prepare a new generation to lead our schools will make a significant difference in the quality of K–12 leadership in public education. Within the following chapters, you will find a mixture of craft knowledge and research focused on improving practice for the novice and experienced principal.

How does a principal bring a new vision to a school without destroying the visions of those professionals who came before? Is it possible for change to occur while at the same time developing and maintaining collaborative relationships between the staff and principal? What are the necessary ingredients for improving a school culture while, at the same time, building trusting relationships between the principal and teacher?

Phyllis A. Gimbel's research provides vivid vignettes and helpful research on the challenges connected to being a competent, trusted school leader. She uses her personal experiences as well as anecdotes from friends and colleagues to tell a compelling story. Her data is evidence of how schools of education and principal internships should rewrite the playbook on the principalship. It is no longer acceptable to send well-meaning aspiring principals out into the world without equipping them with the proper tools to do the work personally as well as technically. Principals cannot survive if teachers and staff do not believe in their leadership. Phyllis gets to the core issue, which is, what it takes to create a school of believers.

Most new principals will be mandated to make change in the schools they will lead. Too many public school educators are in danger of failing the children whose education is entrusted to them. To get the job done will require leaders capable of enlisting teachers, staff, and the community in the quest to prepare every child with a quality education. I recommend this book to all who want to be challenged, entertained, and enlightened and most importantly to all who will accept the calling of becoming a school principal.

> Milli Pierce, Ed.D.
> Director, The Principals' Center
> Harvard Graduate School of Education

PREFACE

In his 1990 book *Improving Schools from Within,* Roland S. Barth writes, "Unfortunately, things between teachers and principals have become increasingly strained with growing emphasis on teacher empowerment, pupil minimum competency, collective bargaining, declines in student population, reduction in teacher force, increased litigation and, above all, 'accountability'" (pp. 19–20).

Today, not much has changed regarding the constraints on principal–teacher relationships. In fact, the growing emphasis on both principal and teacher accountability augments the problems of trust building between the principal and the teaching staff. Principals evaluate teachers and as long as this arrangement continues, principals will need to find ways to build trust with their teachers.

The evolution of this book came from my own experience as a principal. Having spent many years in the classroom, the transition to principal meant doing something I had never done before: working hard at building trusting relationships with teachers. I am an extravert, someone who is invited to parties because I feel comfortable making new friends, making conversation, and understanding how other people feel. I never had a problem relating to people, professionally or personally.

Then I became a principal. In Massachusetts, principals are not part of collective bargaining. I was no longer part of the cohort of teachers with whom I joked and shared pedagogy in the teachers' lounge. I could no longer walk into the faculty lounge and partake in discussion. Whenever I entered the faculty lounge, teachers stopped talking.

This change in the way others treated me gnawed at me. I felt uneasy in my daily practice, always wondering how I was being perceived. The greatest part of my time as principal was spent in an almost endless series of encounters, from the moment I arrived at school until the moment I left. Most of these encounters were face to face, tending to keep me in a highly personal role. I wondered if teachers knew I was sincere. Did they value my open, honest nature? Did they understand that I was trying to be responsive to their needs? Did they trust me?

As a new principal in charge of creating a new middle school, trust was of utmost importance. To effect change in my school, I needed to have faculty trust. Teachers needed to know that I understood all that was expected of them and that I valued their professionalism. As principal, I needed to count on teachers to help implement policies that I felt were important. I knew that as the symbolic head of the school organization, I was the most important individual in the school in developing an atmosphere of trust.

Since I was enrolled in a doctoral program in leadership in schooling, I decided to pilot a brief survey about trust. So in the second year of my tenure as principal, I asked teachers how they felt I was doing in building trusting relationships with them. Their feedback sparked my thinking about this topic and later became the impetus for this book.

ACKNOWLEDGMENTS

I would especially like to thank my daughter, Emilie Gimbel Schnitman, an extremely insightful educator and fine writer herself, for the pertinent, objective comments she offered on the manuscript.

I also would also like to thank Drs. John F. LeBaron, Joyce Taylor Gibson, and Charles (Chuck) Christensen for their guidance during my doctoral studies. Without their collective expertise, I would not have been able to conceive the idea for this book. It was Dr. LeBaron who suggested the topic of trust in schools as "something worthy" of publication.

Scarecrow Education managing editor Cindy Tursman put up with my questions and I appreciate her valuable input. Dr. Susan Villani served as a mentor in the initial stages of this book. Her advice was also invaluable.

INTRODUCTION

Trust is built by learning to depend on the principal, as school leader, as a "broker" to respond to needs of the teachers for resources, classroom management tips and overall being there for teachers which allow them to do their job.

—Middle school teacher

Trust is precarious, it can be lost overnight.

—Middle school principal

"Why can't we have more social studies books? This is ridiculous, using 1983 texts in 1998 and not being able to have enough textbooks for all students. Did you really try to get the books for us?" one of the eighth grade teachers asked me, the new principal of the newly established middle school.

I looked around at the crumbling building: the paint-chipped walls, the pitted concrete entrance steps, the twenty-four broken window panes, the rotted wooden window sills, the water-stained ceilings, the ceilings with missing acoustic tiles exposing the 1948 lead pipes, the dark corridors, the filthy, worn, dull, dark brown, linoleum floor tiles, the exposed electric outlets that were missing brass protective covers, the unlit exit signs, the corroded auditorium curtains, the window shades stuck in the up position, and the fifty-year-old blackboards dulled by erasures.

Then I listened to the teachers complaining about not having enough graphing calculators, pencils and pens, not having access to PA announcements because of broken speakers, not having computer access, and having broken desks, tables, and chairs. I listened to teachers lament that there were not enough trained special education teachers and aides for the implementation of the inclusion program. I listened to staff complain that the district was not providing enough professional development programs for teacher recertification. Teachers said that other school districts offered more professional development training. I listened to teachers remark that they had too many duties and not enough time to meet together.

I was trying so hard to be empathic, to listen and to care. I thought by listening and then expressing openly how disappointed I felt about the lack of teacher resources, teachers would begin to trust me. I told them how I was advocating for them, trying to get whatever resources possible. My proposed new budget reflected care and concern for the teachers. I thought I was building relationships and thereby building trust.

Just how important is building trust? Studies by Professor John O. Whitney, the director of the W. Edwards Deming Quality Center, show that up to 50 percent of work time is often wasted due to lack of trust (Cooper, 1997).

As a new middle school principal working in an all white, blue-collar, seaside community, I was not sure what I had or had not been doing to demonstrate my trust in teachers. Having been hired with a mandate to build a middle school, merging two distinct faculties and hiring a third more new teachers to the total staff, I wanted my teachers to know that I cared about them, that I supported and trusted them. I also wanted to know if they trusted me. My experience was informing me that mutual trust was important to our ability to collaborate and share ideas and thoughts about better ways to educate middle school students. Although trust is important at any level, I knew that in the middle school it is critical for teachers and principals to reflect a united effort, displaying care and concern for young adolescents.

I was worried. Worried because I had been working publicly and privately to blend two distinct faculties who had been transferred involuntarily to a middle school, from a high school and an elementary school. In trying to be as fair and open as possible, I thought I was working hard to meet the individual and collective needs of the teachers.

Whenever a problem surfaced, I met with the teacher. I was spending a great portion of the school day with individual teachers. I confronted uncomfortable situations with teachers, students, and parents. Aware that these teachers had been forced to this school and that they had a new principal, I focused on understanding the teachers' perspective.

Prior to concluding my second year as principal, I wanted to know more about building relationships with teachers, if teachers trusted me, and if they knew I trusted them. I wanted to know if my behaviors inspired trust in me as principal. I knew there were several more middle school initiatives to implement and faculty trust would be needed. I wanted to know if what I was perceiving as trustworthy behaviors were the same behaviors that the faculty viewed as trust enhancers. So I conducted a pilot study, surveying teachers about how trust is built between the middle school principal and teachers. The responses clustered around specific behaviors that promoted trust in me, as principal, and around some of my actions that seemed to deter trust building between the teaching staff and myself as principal.

While categorizing data from my pilot study, it became apparent that certain data indicated specific dimensions of what trust looked like at my school. I wondered if these dimensions of interpersonal trust would be the same in other public schools. I also wondered if I would have been able to achieve more on behalf of my students and teachers if I had known earlier in my tenure about how to build trust. My pilot study served as an impetus for this book and prompted the following questions: What constitutes trust? What kind of behaviors of the principal promote trust between the principal and teaching staff?

In response to these questions, this book contains seven chapters. In chapter 1, I explore leader behavior and trust, trust and principal–teacher relationships, and why trust in schools is important. In chapter 2, I examine principal and teacher perceptions about the meaning of trust in three schools and suggest some common elements of trust.

In the third chapter, I describe trust-promoting leader behaviors at the three schools, from both the principal and teachers' perspectives. In chapter 4, I consider making sense of these principal–teacher perceptions of trust.

In chapter 5, I look at what all of this means for practitioners by creating a list of what I call "trust enhancers." Using these specific behaviors could help current and aspiring school leaders to focus on trust-building behaviors. I also offer some suggestions about hiring principals and modifying principal training programs.

Chapter 6 contains some thoughts about the relevance of promoting trust in the current atmosphere of legislated school reform. Finally, chapter 7 recaps the list of trust enhancers and highlights some practices in which they might be useful.

①

STRUGGLES IN FOSTERING TRUSTING PRINCIPAL–TEACHER RELATIONSHIPS

"**I**nstead of the traditional Christmas tree," Jean announced at the second faculty meeting in her tenure as elementary school principal, "we are going to have a wishing well, where kids can bring gifts for the needy."

"Is she crazy?" several teachers muttered. "We have had a Christmas tree here for twenty-five years," they explained. "You can't do that," the building representative for the teachers' union declared. "All of us have contributed ornaments over the years and we look forward to the tree. Parents and kids love to come to our school during the holidays because we decorate so beautifully."

"I've given a lot of thought to this and some of our students are Jehovah's Witnesses and they do not celebrate Christmas. Others are Jewish and Muslim. Some kids are so poor they cannot give or receive gifts. Therefore, I don't think we should have a tree," Jean said.

The week after the faculty meeting, Jean found an article in the local newspaper, recounting her decision about not to have a tree. The article was entitled "New Elementary Principal Does Not Allow Christmas Tree." Several teachers, including the building union representative, were quoted as saying the new principal did not honor local traditions and that she made a quick decision without consulting teachers.

A few days after the article appeared in the small, local newspaper, a reporter from a larger regional newspaper called to interview Jean. She agreed to the interview. When the article appeared in his newspaper, it stated that the first thing Jean tackled as the new principal was the Christmas tree. The article went on to say that the teachers were stupefied by Jean's mandate.

Ten days after the regional paper ran the article, a television reporter contacted Jean. He said that the union president had called him to say that the town's new elementary principal had only been in the school for two months and, without discussion, had taken something away from the teachers that was very dear to them, a symbol of local tradition. He wanted to interview Jean, highlighting one school leader's personal crusade to follow her vision. Jean refused the interview.

How such a school incident could become magnified to this degree seems odd, when the recent focus is on raising student achievement. But improving student achievement requires a school culture wherein there is faculty trust in the principal. How a principal acts determines how he or she engenders faculty trust in the principal. Principals like Jean portray a vivid picture of how a principal's behavior impacts the process of building trusting principal–teacher relationships.

TRUST AND PRINCIPAL–TEACHER RELATIONSHIPS

Let's explore what might have led to Jean's decision and how she could have handled it differently to foster teacher trust. Having just graduated from a top tier school of education, Jean felt imbued with a sense of how to run an effective school. The daughter of a Protestant minister, Jean agreed with the current tenet of access and equity for all children, socially and academically. One of the reasons she wanted to become a principal was to put into practice the values she had acquired while growing up and while studying at a highly respected school of education. So doing away with a Christmas tree seemed like increasing equity for the diverse student population in Jean's new elementary school. How could Jean have acted to promote a relationship of interpersonal trust with her teaching staff that would have given more effect to her vision? What is the meaning of trust in schools?

Perhaps Jean had not reflected on how her behavior would impact relationships between herself and her teaching staff. Maybe she did not realize that the challenge of leadership in schools is to build a trusting relationship between leader and follower. The principal needs to be able to count on teachers to help implement policies that he or she holds to be important.

THE NEED FOR BUILDING ONE-TO-ONE PRINCIPAL–TEACHER RELATIONSHIPS

In spite of the importance of relationships in schools, the current emphasis on school accountability constrains principal–teacher relationships. For more than a decade, there has been a national focus on school improvement that is based on state-mandated testing and curriculum. Schools are now facing extraordinary pressure around accountability for student achievement. This focus on accountability has created principal–teacher anxiety, making it more difficult to foster trusting relationships between principals and teachers. Yet more than ever, principals and teachers need to collaborate to share ideas about student achievement, to raise expectations, and to create communities of learners.

Literature from the 1990s implies that trust rests on the ability of the principal to promote relationships with teachers. Underpinning the research is the notion that the behavior of the principal sets the tone of relationships in school settings. Some studies suggest that much of teacher thinking about trust relates to the expectations teachers have for their principal's behavior in either professional or administrative relationships. As such, teachers tend to focus more on one-to-one relationships with their principal when they think about trusting him or her than they do about the principal's organizational responsibilities. It seems more important to teachers how the principal relates to them professionally than how the school is managed. The message is pretty clear that there is a relationship between the extent of trust and the quality of the interpersonal principal–teacher relationship. As described by teachers and principals in subsequent chapters of this book, the building and sustaining of one-to-one relationships with teachers via communicative and supportive behaviors is the overarching trust-promoting behavior of the principal. This type of leader behavior may look like common sense, but it is far from common practice.

LEADER BEHAVIOR AND TRUST

The current school improvement mandate urges principals to find ways to develop teacher loyalty, trust, and motivation. To lead, the principal has to have informal authority and a key to the development of such influence is the principal's ability to generate faculty trust. But how? Are there specific behaviors, policies, or practices of the principal that promote faculty trust? Do the principal and teachers perceive trust in the same way? Learning to lead requires behaving in a way that fosters relationship building.

It seems easy to say that an honest, authentic leader can promote a climate of trust, but teachers are in a subordinate position and often fear authority. This process of leading is an attempt to influence the behavior of others to motivate them to do things differently. Therefore, they tend to base their behavior on power and distrust rather than on trust and intimacy. Sometimes, people talk glibly about how simple it is to build trust, but it is another matter to define and explain exactly how it evolves between principals and their teaching staffs. This book serves as a resource to principals and other school leaders who want to make the building of trust an explicit goal by focusing on behaviors of the principal that are enhancing rather than inhibiting. This book examines principals' and teachers' perceptions about the meaning of trust.

Head of the school organization, the principal probably is the single most important individual in developing an atmosphere of trust. As organizational leader, the principal is responsible for creating conditions of trust because of control of its determinants. Yet, what the principal perceives as a trust-building behavior may not be what teachers perceive. This possible dissonance of perception is relevant to defining and fostering faculty trust in the principal.

As defined by principals and teachers, trust appears, in part, to mean something slightly different, contingent on the setting. There is little systematic research on trust in public schools. The examination of trust is problematic because many models of trust tend to be very vague and inexact. This book discusses what trust means to teachers and principals within their own school settings. The perceptions of principals and teachers, however, do provide a knowledge base of specific "trust enhancers," allowing readers to see the virtues of some discrete leader behaviors and to gain an understanding of the meaning of trust in schools.

PROMOTING TRUSTING PRINCIPAL-TEACHER RELATIONSHIPS

In her third year of tenure, Paula wanted to obtain a better grasp of what was actually being taught in the classrooms. Although she evaluated twenty-three new teachers several times throughout the school year, there were another twenty teachers in her middle school who, according to union contract, were not to be evaluated during the current school year. Paula did walk around the school building as often as possible, but she could not spend as much time in all the classrooms as she desired.

Formerly a high school department chair, Paula knew that collecting teachers' plan books every two weeks was one way of monitoring curriculum and instruction. So she went to her School Governance Council. The School Governance Council, an advisory group, was composed of team leaders from every grade level team, the school psychologist, and a representative from the special education and related arts teachers. Paula discussed her idea of collecting lesson plan books every other week and her rationale for doing so. Teacher representatives to the council said they would talk about it at their team meetings and would get back to Paula before the next governance meeting.

The next governance meeting was attended not only by the regular members, but by ten additional teachers. Paula had prepared an agenda for the meeting and when it was time for discussion about lesson plan collection, many teacher hands were raised. Several teachers expressed excitement about sharing their plans, saying that no principal had ever looked at their plan books. They expressed content at being able to share their work with the principal.

By contrast, the art teacher displayed concern. "How will you judge my plans? I don't have a specific format. I sometimes sketch out what I want the students to do," the art teacher stammered. Her question seemed to inspire another concern, one that was raised by the music teacher who was also the union president. "I don't write lesson plans. I never have and I do not intend to change the way I plan for my classes," the music teacher declared. "Did Paula say we needed to have a certain format?" inquired John, a seventh grade history teacher.

"No, I did not specify a deliberate format, but I did enumerate that I would like to see the state standards that are being addressed in each lesson or activity," Paula clarified.

"Oh, that is fine," Lucy, the eighth grade language arts teacher replied. "By doing that, I will myself be able to monitor the language arts curriculum," she added.

Beth, the music teacher/union president, continued, "I am not going to do that. My teaching is spontaneous. I know what I have to cover when and if the kids are not in the mood for what I have planned. I don't want to be held to what I write in a plan book."

"Thank you for being honest, Beth," Paula replied. "This is precisely why we are discussing this in Governance Council first, before I put this on the next faculty meeting agenda. I understand what you are saying, especially in light of the moodiness of middle school–age youngsters. It is always wise to write your lesson plans in pencil. Then, you are not beholden to them. I am not looking for a beautiful looking book, only the lesson objective, the activities to support it, and the connection to the state's academic standards. It does not matter if you cross out, erase, or write in the margin," Paula explained.

"Well, I will think about it. But if I change my plan in the book, I will have to rewrite the objective and everything else," Beth complained. "By the way, Paula, are you going to use our lesson plan books to evaluate us? If so, that needs to be impact bargained," the union leader stated.

"No, I never intended to do that, Beth. You know my rationale for collecting the books," Paula replied. "About your other concern, Beth, if you do not accomplish what you write in the plan book, I am willing to let you submit an alternative lesson plan when I collect the book two weeks later. I would rather not do it that way, but maybe to start, it would be okay like that."

Two weeks later, at the full faculty meeting, Paula brought this issue up for teacher discussion. Most of the teachers had already heard from their colleagues about Paula's new initiative of collecting plan books bi-weekly. Although they felt it would be more work, almost all of the math, science, social studies, language arts, health, and foreign language teachers agreed to Paula's initiative. The art, music, and physical education teachers objected. They claimed they did not write lesson plans.

"I understand that this is new for you," Paula told the related arts teachers, "but I am willing to be tolerant of your own format for your plans. Let's give it a try for two months and then revisit this issue to see where we are."

"Okay," the music teacher/union president replied. We will try for two months. That is four plan book collections."

This case about Paula, a middle school principal in her third year of tenure, differs from that of Jean, an elementary principal in the first few months of her principalship. Paula seemed to know not to initiate something completely new in the first few months of her first year of tenure. Why did she know that and Jean did not? Paula did impose more work on the teachers and especially on those teachers, like the music teacher/union president and the art teacher, who did not write lesson plans. Paula knew that, but figured out a way to implement a new practice. How did she behave to get teachers to cooperate with her?

This book examines the perceptions of principals and teachers about what they think are barriers to promoting trusting relationships between themselves and about what types of leader behaviors engender faculty trust in the principal. By reading what practitioners say about trust and relationship building, current and aspiring principals can channel their behaviors, practices, and policies to elicit a solid, trusting rapport with their teaching staffs.

WHY TRUST IN SCHOOLS IS IMPORTANT

All this talk about trust does not seem meaningful until circumstances occur in a school setting wherein the concept of trust seems important. Sometimes, principals who are new to their schools walk into school buildings that are devoid of trust. They may feel the school has a very cold climate and that the perceptions of administrators are suspicious and negative. Such school leaders need some data to guide them in working with their faculties. They know that in order to raise test scores, teachers may need to modify instruction. How could they motivate their teaching staffs to expand their repertoires of pedagogical skills?

Principals who feel this way and those mentioned elsewhere in this chapter are everywhere. Such school leaders want to effect change for democratic governance in schools, to restructure or to improve schools, to implement policies, to raise expectations, to create communities of learners, to build team spirit to collaborate and share ideas about student achievement, to pursue common goals, to maintain effective communication for good supervision, to grow professionally as teachers and principals, and to display a united effort for students by building relationships. These school leaders want to establish conditions under which it is possible for their staffs to trust them. Principals and other administrators want to know how to acquire their teachers' trust so that their faculties know they are operating in the school's best interest. Based on my experience as a teacher, department chair, principal, and researcher, I believe that the substance of interpersonal trust in schools is rooted in the behavior of principals.

In chapter 2, I discuss the meaning of trust in schools. The discussion revolves around the perceptions of teachers and principals from different public schools. I describe the dissonance and convergence of definitions of the substance of interpersonal trust in schools. The meaning of trust as it relates to teachers and principals within their own school settings will be examined.

2

PRINCIPAL AND TEACHER PERCEPTIONS ABOUT THE MEANING OF TRUST IN SCHOOLS

Interest in the trust-building process grew during my own tenure as principal. In order to corroborate some of my own experiences in trust building, I visited three public middle schools to talk about trust with principals and teachers. At each school, I met individually with the principal and then with small focus groups of teachers. Contingent on the school setting, trust appeared to mean something slightly different in each school. Yet, some common elements of trust emerged, which I later categorize according to the perspective of each principal and each group of teachers. To contextualize the principal–teacher perceptions of trust, the following are descriptions of each school and each principal.

CHEERFUL MIDDLE SCHOOL

Cheerful Middle School, built in 1973, has recently been renovated and boasts new, speckled, white vinyl floors; bright blue, freshly painted, cinder block walls; new carpeting in designated areas of the school; and a half-million dollars' worth of technology. There are no graffiti on the walls or anywhere else in the school building. There is a quilt hanging from the front entryway wall. The quilt says "Our Country Our Heritage." Classrooms are equipped with television (TV) monitors so that morning announcements may be televised throughout the school. Channel 10 runs the school's PowerPoint events of the day and is updated daily by the secretary. TV monitors, located in various corridors throughout the building, portray the daily happenings. Channel 19 is reserved for classroom teachers to run videos programmed from the special technology equipment room, where there are four videocassette recorders hooked into the school network. As reflected in the district's commitment to technology and the principal's desire to use computers and video, the school has 100 percent of its classrooms on the Internet.

The imposing, three-story, brick school building is situated on a residential street about five miles from main state highways. There is a country club on the same street. The school is set back from the road by a long driveway, a large faculty and staff parking lot, and spacious lawns.

Currently, Cheerful Middle School houses 714 students in grades six to eight. The faculty includes fifty-five teachers. According to the Massachusetts Department of Education, this school is 90 percent white and there are no limited English-proficient students.

Cheerful's principal, Brad, is a stately, tall, brown-haired, middle-aged man, who usually wears a jacket, white shirt, and a Save the Children neck tie. His sensible, butterscotch-colored, rubber-soled, tie shoes are loosely tied with dark brown laces and his necktie is flung around his neck. His hair is neatly combed on one side of his head, but the other side is disheveled.

Holding a doctorate in education, Brad has been a principal in this school for two and half years and was a middle school principal and technology director beforehand. He said that technology is his great love and that he was very fortunate to work in a system that had allocated funds to technology prior to his tenure as principal here. He explained that among the schools in the town, his was the only school that conducted daily business via telecommunications. Brad distributes school newsletters and all communications via the Internet. His bimonthly newsletters also appear in hard copy for those families who still do not have Internet access. Any messages for teachers are sent via e-mail.

In 1993, Brad was elected Principal of the Year by the local affiliate of the National Association of Secondary School Principals. One of the sole decorative objects in Brad's tiny, brick-walled, oblong office is a trophy attesting to the honor bestowed on him. Brad's office is located near the main entrance to the building, allowing him a view of the comings and goings near the main entrance.

On the first visit to Cheerful, Brad volunteered a tour of the school building. During the tour, several teachers and students saw Brad in the hall and came to greet him. They exchanged dialogue about daily happenings and about events in their personal lives. Most of the classroom doors throughout the three levels of the building were open and Brad dashed in and out of classrooms. No one seemed to notice his presence. One or two teachers offered to apprise Brad about what was going on in the class and two or three students said hello to him. In the computer class, students were inputting data about their recently elevated scores on the state-mandated testing, the Massachusetts Comprehensive Assessment System (MCAS). The school's scores indicated a rise since Brad stepped in almost three years ago. The colorful, student-made, Excel spreadsheets from this class were reminiscent of the large data chart at the school entrance, which portrayed the dramatic rise in test scores and Cheerful's improved state rating.

Cheerful Principal's Perception of Trust

Authenticity   "If I had to define interpersonal trust, I would say it is the perception on behalf of the staff that I, the principal, articulate what I am about as an educator, as a principal of a middle school, what my goals are, what my expectations are for those people and that my behavior flows and follows what I say I believe in and what I say I expect those people to do and what I say myself to do with this follow-through." Brad added a few more dimensions of trust, and defined them as authenticity, honesty, and intuition. He provided examples of these dimensions by specifying, "If I say that it's important to be a good communicator, that I walk the talk so to speak, and communicate as effectively as I can and have the same expectations that the staff do the same thing. . . . So, the trust has to do with believing that you are what you are and you do what you say."

Brad spoke about using his intuition to figure out which of his teachers had trust in him. He claimed that if he saw teachers "going the extra mile," his "assumption is that they have trust in me."

Attitude   Brad pointed to a "positive way" that teachers acted when he would "make demands on them." He claimed that this positive teacher attitude was an indication of a trusting relationship between the teachers and himself. He further articulated, "I believe in basic trust in all staff and I start with that concept—that you want to do this job, that you are a professional . . . so I don't dwell on the negative side." Brad suggested that he, as principal, also maintained a positive attitude toward teachers.

Cheerful Teachers' Perception of Trust

Authenticity   The Cheerful teachers with whom I met felt strongly that the meaning of trust between themselves and their principal meant that Brad was honest with them and that they were honest with him. "I believe that honesty is an important consideration. I'm more honest and I expect that other teachers are honest and that our Principal is honest. Those are probably common occurrences in working relationships." As a part of honesty, teachers felt that follow-through was important in defining trust. Several teachers commented, "How the principal responds to that honesty affects the relationship that happens or doesn't happen." The teachers said that they expected Brad to follow-through consistently. Brad's follow-through demonstrated an expression of teacher trust in him and his trust in them. This idea bordered on what teachers expressed as mutual involvement. "A third factor I would mention is mutual involvement as an indication of trust. I'm willing to get involved at his request and he is willing to get involved at my request," one of the teachers explained.

Support   A common definition of trust among this group of teachers was maintaining confidentiality. One of the teachers expressed this by saying, "If I speak with Brad about a situation, whether it is a personal situation, a classroom situation, or a coworker situation, I would expect that he would be able to treat it with great confidentiality." Another Cheerful teacher said that she was "looking for support and recognition of the work" that she put into the school. That recognition, she claimed, indicated trust. A third teacher stated that "the principal's interest in you as a teacher and in the goals of the school and students" were important in establishing a trusting principal–

teacher relationship. To stretch this idea further, a teacher stated that "our principal seeks out information from other people when he does not have the expertise himself. He will ask the opinion of people who are specialists in that field and I find that I appreciate that very much, that he trusts the opinions of people who are experts in that field and will fully back that position because he trusts his staff and he has reason to."

Another teacher added that respect is a component of trust and a dimension of support in that "trust builds respect and respect builds into trust between the principal and the teachers." The final aspect of trust as support, then, according to these teachers, is the fairness of their principal in treating all teachers equally. A teacher commented, "Not always do you get what you want from Brad, but the situation is treated appropriately and everything is the same for everybody. There are no favorites."

The principal and teachers at Cheerful Middle School perceived trust as being mutually honest, authentic, communicative, and supportive with the ultimate goal of developing and sustaining relationships. Cheerful teachers specified maintaining confidentiality as a supportive indication of interpersonal trust.

HANDY MIDDLE SCHOOL

Set back from a quiet, quasi-rural, winding street, just a few minutes from the exit of a major highway, on a private driveway sits the imposing, two-story brick Handy Middle School. The white-and-black lettered wooden sign to the school is attached to a painted, white colonial post. The style of the sign matches that of nearby houses, colonial and rustic. In keeping with the rural flavor of the community, there is a great deal of wide open space and playing fields next to the school. Some of the houses on the street are farmhouses built in the 1860s and 1870s and others are new developments of large homes. The houses are spaced quite far apart, some allowing land for horses to roam between the fences separating farms and new homes.

From the outside, several classroom windows are covered with decorative, snowflake cutouts. At the main entrance to the school hangs a banner reading, "Success . . . Choose it." The main entrance is spacious, a place where students wait for their parents to pick them up, congregate between classes, or wait for late buses. The platform of the main entryway is made of stone to absorb the winter slush, snow, and ice drippings from students' shoes and boots. The flooring for the rest of the building is the same as that of Cheerful Middle School, white linoleum, speckled with an occasional, dark green, vinyl tile. The school was just renovated and, in fact, construction was not yet finished.

The principal's office is located adjacent to the main entryway. Next to his office is the new assistant principal's office. Both offices are painted a bright, cheerful mint green and have windows facing the front of the school.

Handy Middle School includes 850 students in grades five to eight and has a faculty of 77 full- and part-time teachers and specialists. The Massachusetts Department of Education statistics point to a white student population of 98.9 percent and no limited English-proficient students. One hundred percent of the classrooms are connected to the Internet within the school. The principal reports that there is no use of Intranet, as the office computers are not linked to the classrooms.

Handy's impeccably groomed and well-dressed principal, Tony, has served as principal for seven and a half years. While touring the school with Tony, several classroom doors were open and Tony entered the rooms, offering some brief dialogue. During the break between classes, a few teachers stood in the halls. Three or four of them remarked that Tony was an excellent principal and that there was "a lot of trust" in the school. In two of the classes, art and music, students appeared excited to be interacting with the teacher and with one another. Huddled in small groups, students worked collaboratively on projects. Tony praised the art and music teachers.

Tony discussed with me the tension he had been under because of the ongoing renovation of the school. He mentioned there was a blackout in September of the current school year, which caused some electrical problems in the building. He also explained that air quality had been a problem during the renovation project and that he felt that his trust level with the teachers was different from what it had been prior to the renovations.

Handy Principal's Perception of Trust

Availability   According to Tony, trust meant developing and sustaining relationships with teachers by being available to them. Tony explained how he thought he had developed trusting relationships with teachers. He said, "The teachers see me in the halls, in the mornings, at lunch time, and I tend to talk a lot informally. I'm in classrooms everyday. Teachers are very comfortable with me being in their classes while they're teaching. . . . The more they see me, the more there is trust."

In Tony's eyes, the practice of being visible around the school and not in his office was a factor in establishing trusting relationships. Trust also meant honesty. He explained that he deliberately tried to engage teachers in conversation about school issues whenever he saw them, no matter where they were in the building. "Teachers are very aware that I'm around the building all the time and so there are no symbolic blocks to communication because I'm around and about most of the time." Tony implied that trust was being visible to teachers, reassuring them that he was there for them.

Authenticity   When asked what trust between himself and his teaching staff meant, Tony replied, "Well, I believe that trust is a matter of being honest with the teachers and I would say that includes . . . following through about particular issues that teachers are concerned about. He further remarked, "I think the ultimate trust in this business is that teachers know their principals are teachers first and they can teach and they can walk the talk."

Tony emphasized the value of his teaching staff seeing him work hard so that they would know he was "working hard for them." He also stressed the importance of teachers seeing him in the role of a teacher, to make him someone the teachers could trust because he understood the nature of their work.

Tony was honest about his weaknesses to his staff, "I tend to be a conceptual person and look for some assistance for details and the devil's in the details for all of us, and yes, that's the way I have always been. I'm a global person. I like the goals. I like this and that strength-wise, but I need all the help I can get with a master schedule and the finite details and I struggle with that on a day-to-day basis. And people know this, so sometimes I think that the fact that I know this about myself impacts on trust," Tony added, acknowledging his strengths and shortcomings.

Communication   Tony conceptualized honest, open dialogue as a dimension of the meaning of trust between himself and his teachers. "I started off in this school interviewing teachers on a one-to-one basis over the summer. . . . I continue to talk informally with teachers and I think if I brought anything to this school it is informal dialogue with people about important issues." "This," he said, "is part of the meaning of trust."

Tony also pointed out, "It is important that I am open and honest in my communication in what my job entails and that I communicate that to the teachers on a one-to-one basis, in an informal way, whenever the opportunity arises." As we continued our conversation, Tony said that he tried to be available to meet with teachers as needed.

Tony talked a little more deliberately when he explained how important one-to-one relationships with teachers were in the trust-building process. He recognized that trusting relationships rested on communication of what the challenges of the principal's job were and also on his becoming acquainted with the faculty as individuals. Tony's entry plan into the school, seven and half years ago, included one-to-one interviews with the teachers so that he knew something about each of them and that they knew something about him.

Handy Teachers' Perceptions of Trust

Authenticity   "I would say that in terms of anything else about the relationship of trust, I think it's an intuitive thing, that we simply do not have a sense of knowing that someone is watching over us all the time." The teachers with whom I spoke suspected a feeling of being trusted by Tony.

"I think that the principal needs to trust himself in order to have trust between himself and us," the Handy Middle School teachers commented. They thought that the principal trusted those people he hired because, they claimed, he had an intuition that he could trust them.

"Our principal," they added, "is open and honest, that's his style. He admits his weaknesses to us. For example, he does not mind being reminded ten times that he needs to do something because he knows he is not good with details." This honesty, they conjectured, was a dimension of interpersonal trust.

Communication   A veteran teacher explained what trust between teachers and her principal looked like. "Tony took the time, when he was first hired, to meet with every single one of his staff members before school opened. These meetings continued within an extremely short time afterward. He basically picked our brains. . . . And I think he wanted to know where we had come from and where we were before he decided about trying to take us where we needed to go." The teachers alluded to this one-to-one interchange as part of the meaning of trust in that their principal had an opportunity to know them and for them to know him. The Handy teachers affirmed that Tony visited their classes and walked the corridors of the school. In this way, they claimed, he talked with them informally, often on a one-to-one basis. Teachers said that Tony "hits things head on. He calls us to chat with him about certain issues and involves us in some of his decision making. He works collegially. Our principal puts problems on the table and asks how we can resolve them together."

"From the beginning of his tenure," the Handy teachers said, "Tony articulated his expectations of his staff." One Handy teacher declared, "I know we have a relationship of trust. Tony made it clear up front." Another teacher remembered Tony saying, "This is how I deal with my staff and you're not going to see me looking over your shoulder at every moment to see what's going on in your room. You will be on your own to be a professional. I hired you as a professional, you are a professional." Teachers expressed pleasure that their principal was very clear with them about his confidence in their professionalism. He told them when they did something "good."

Support   One of the Handy Middle School teachers said, "I think, first of all, trust has to be built. I don't think there is any question about that, but basically when it exists, it means that there is confidence on both sides that the jobs we're hired to do are being done. There is a sense that you don't have to look over people's shoulders all the time and that things will go along smoothly because everybody's on the same wave length in terms of what's being done and this is being done so that things go along without inordinate glitches. Things that you could predict. You have to have a certain faith in the individual as a person as well as in the role as the principal. I think if there isn't any faith in the person, it's very hard to trust the person in the role. . . . So trust is faith, the same beliefs and confidence in each person to do the job that has to be done."

Another teacher substantiated this feeling of interpersonal trust when she uttered, "Our principal does not look over our shoulder. He hired us because he thinks we are capable. He allows us the space to do our job. We know this is trust."

These teachers connected trust between themselves and their principal through his abilities to maintain confidentiality and to respect them. "I define trust with my principal the same way I define it with anyone else. That is, if I share something with someone, I expect it to be confidential, and I mind if it is shared with other people. . . . I do trust him and I trust him implicitly, to be honest with you. And I trust his judgment, which I think has to go with trust. Judgment and trust go together so I think you need to know someone before you trust them. You can't trust them blindly. Since our principal took time to get to know us as people as well as professionals, he has an awful lot of faith in his staff," a teacher noted. A teacher new to this school added, "He made it clear to me in the beginning, that he hired professionals whom he trusted to carry out what they needed to do within the classrooms. So he does not have an overseeing type of relationship with us and he respects us." "Yes," chimed in another teacher, "confidence has a lot to do with the meaning of trust. He has confidence in me. I have confidence in him, in the aspect of I know if there was ever an issue with a parent he would be behind me one hundred percent, so there's a trust issue."

From the perspectives of the Handy Middle School principal and the teachers, trust meant that the principal made himself available to develop and sustain relationships with teachers by maintaining authenticity and communicating and supporting teachers. For teachers, trust meant that their principal supported them by respecting their professionalism and maintaining their confidentiality.

WESTERN MIDDLE SCHOOL

Western Middle School is situated on Main Street, across from the Haitian Methodist Church, an Italian restaurant, an insurance company, a chiropractor, and a fire station built in 1890. A Chinese restaurant is one block from the school. Western Middle School was constructed in 1923 and an addition was constructed in 1976, which included a gym. There are no playing fields outside the school, as the only area surrounding the building is a small, inadequate, unpaved, parking lot for staff and faculty. Western Middle School is a brick, slate-roofed building, three stories high.

The main entrance to the school, on Main Street, is locked and no longer provides access to the school. The former main entrance is majestic, composed of several, large double doors at the top of some elongated, concrete steps. The current, single-door entrance is on a side street, facing narrow, two-story, single-family dwellings. In order to enter the school, a visitor rings a buzzer and speaks into an intercom connected to the main office. The school secretary identifies the visitor and then, if satisfied with the caller, hits a buzzer that opens the door automatically.

The school is clean, with no graffiti anywhere. Every inch of space is utilized. Even the part-time school psychologist works in a closet under a stairwell. Western houses 380 students in grades six to eight and contains a faculty of 67 full- and part-time teachers and aides.

According to the Massachusetts Department of Education statistics, Western Middle School is 10 percent African American, 6 percent Asian, 10 percent Hispanic, and 74 percent white. Despite these figures, there are no limited English-proficient students. Western has 71 percent of the classrooms on the Internet, with no office connection to other computers in the building.

According to Nathan, the principal of Western Middle School, a new middle school will be built with six hundred to seven hundred students in Western Town, so that there will be two middle schools with approximately the same-size populations. Currently, the other middle school in town is larger because there is no more space in this school.

Nathan is average height, with gray hair and blue eyes. He dresses in a jacket and necktie with a lightly starched, light blue, button-down shirt. His neck shirt button is unbuttoned under his necktie. Nathan appeared proud of his school when he toured the building, he smiled as he encountered several teachers along the way who engaged him in professional conversations. One of the teachers requested that Nathan visit her class so that she could show him what her sixth grade students were writing. This teacher worked in a team next to another teacher who also wanted to say "hello" to Nathan and have him visit his students. Classes were small, with sixteen students in each of the sixth grades. Nathan explained that the classes had to be small because the school building was old and the classrooms were tiny.

When Nathan entered the cafeteria, the ladies who were working there were happy to see him. When Nathan walked up the stairs, the industrial arts teacher asked him about using a tripod and videotaping equipment for a project. Nathan said yes. As he was touring the three-story building, Nathan walked randomly into classrooms, where most of the doors were open, to quickly say "Hi," or to see what was going on. Students, mainly seated in rows, appeared engaged and were listening to the teacher, who stood at the front of the classroom.

Nathan's tiny office is located in a closet-like space, off of the main office. His office contains one large, double-pane window, with a large, vinyl window shade and a window air conditioner. None of the school's entrances are visible from his office. Nathan's office is decorated with a multitude of family photos and photos of former students. The office is very neat, with a large desk and chair, a computer and printer, a few shelves for school-related information, and a bulletin board filled with school and district notices. Everything from the main office is audible from Nathan's office. The PA system is directly in front of his vented, wooden door.

This is Nathan's sixth year in this school. He was an assistant principal in Western Town High School for twenty-three years. Both Nathan and his assistant principal went to Western Middle School as students. Nathan lives three minutes from his school and whenever he jogs, he jogs by the school. Every morning, seven days a week, Nathan enjoys his coffee at a little coffee shop in town. Nathan said that parents and teachers can find him there and call him there whenever they want. Nathan commented about being so familiar with the school system.

Western Principal's Perception of Trust

Reliability   In our conversation, Nathan implied that trust meant reliability. He clarified by saying, "Teachers haven't found many surprises with me and I think that's probably an element of the trust factor. They pretty much know where I'm coming from and they know how I'm going to deal with things. They're not surprised by a reaction that might come out of left field. I try to keep an even keel all the time. They know me by how I react and that is a part of trust." Trust meant that his teachers knew him and knew that he was sincere and was there for them.

Communication   Nathan wrestled with a definition of trust between himself and his teaching staff. He could not quite describe the meaning of interpersonal trust without describing behaviors. "I guess my feeling toward the whole thing would be when people have the faith, and I guess maybe that's the definition, faith to come to you with problems, concerns, issues, and so on and have the belief that you will deal with them on a humane and professional level as opposed to looking at expediency, looking at politics. . . . I guess open, free dialogue is probably part of what I'm looking for. We all have the same beliefs."

Nathan elaborated on the meaning of trust by mentioning more behaviors and not using nouns or phrases that encapsulated the meaning of trust between himself and his teaching staff. When probed about the real meaning of interpersonal trust, Nathan spoke of the value of listening to his teachers as part of the meaning of trust. He said, "I like to feel that there isn't anything that the teaching staff is afraid to tell me, even if they know I'm not going to like hearing it."

The Western Middle School principal emphasized that listening actively to his teaching staff was a large part of his meaning of interpersonal trust. He felt that the listening process constituted a component of the meaning of trust between himself and his faculty. "I like to believe," Nathan commented, "that the teachers know I will respond to their concerns appropriately." Nathan's thoughts about the meaning of trust rested on the premise that he responded and listened consistently and reliably to his teaching staff. His staff placed confidence in him and he did in them. "I think we have to just go ahead and trust. People have to get beyond the issues of motives, they have to believe that we all have the same objective when we come to work in the morning."

Western Teachers' Perception of Trust

Reliability   Like their principal, teachers at Western Middle School focused on behaviors as the meaning of trust. When probed for nouns or descriptive phrases, they still agreed that the meaning of trust between themselves and their principal had to do with being able to count on their principal's consistent reaction and follow-through to what he heard from them. Describing trust in the same terms of their principal, these teachers indicated that their principal had to do something for them in order for them to find meaning in trust. They counted on Nathan's consistent follow-through or his reactions to hearing what they say. "I think that this consistency with him is important, knowing that things don't change is a meaning of trust," a teacher reiterated.

Communication   In this school, the focus on the meaning of trust appeared to be on behaviors and practices rather than on descriptive phrases. One of these teachers commented, "I think that trust is communicating with your principal. . . . I think being listened to is part of trust. Our principal does a good job trying to listen to all of us." Another teacher chimed into the conversation with, "Here, you definitely are listened to." Western teachers equated interpersonal trust with their principal listening to them, giving them information they needed to be effective with students, and following through on things. In referencing Nathan, teachers remarked, "He tells me what's going on, giving me the information that I need to work with the students I work with and when I hear that he really understands my situation, in other words, he knows what's going on in my classroom and he knows what I have to deal with and so when I have a concern about it, he listens to me and acts on it. That's when I know the trust relationship is good between us." Another teacher, who agreed with her colleagues, added that, "I know I can go to him to vent . . . and then I can have a discussion about it afterward and he won't hold me accountable about it afterward. He can keep a confidence. I think this is what trust means for all of us as a group dealing with our principal."

At Western Middle School, the principal and teachers defined trust in terms of actions or behaviors. They described trust quite similarly. Both the teachers and the principal felt that interpersonal trust meant that the principal was reliable, available, and communicative. Like their counterparts at Cheerful and Handy Middle Schools, Western Middle School teachers perceived trust as maintaining confidentiality.

COMMON ELEMENTS OF TRUST

Although the meanings of trust varied slightly for principals at each school site, Brad, Tony, and Nathan shared some common dimensions of trust. All three middle school principals alluded to their own authenticity or sincerity as being a dimension of interpersonal trust. All three administrators focused on developing relationships with teachers as a meaning of trust. All of the principals spoke about their being who they say they are and about following through and being reliable. Brad and Nathan, of Cheerful and Western Middle Schools, respectively, described the meaning of trust between themselves and their teaching staffs as having the same beliefs as their teachers. The principals in Cheerful and Handy schools spoke about honesty as part of the meaning of trust.

All three principals focused on communicating with their teachers. Within this category, however, elements differed. For Handy school principal, Tony, the aspect of communication that defined trust for him was sharing the one-to-one interviews with his staff and sharing the governance of his school. For Nathan of Western Middle School, open, free dialogue, sharing the same beliefs, and active listening were all components of the meaning of trust in terms of communication.

Each of the three principals alluded to aspects of support, in addition to dimensions of communication, as corollaries to their meanings of trust between themselves and their teaching staffs. Cheerful principal, Brad, felt that a positive attitude toward teachers indicated support and trust. Tony, the Handy Middle School principal, perceived being available to teachers for informal dialogue as a meaning of trust. Nathan, the Western Middle School principal, claimed that being available, reliable, and responsive meant trust.

Consistent with the three principals, there was overlap in the meaning of trust in one category for teachers in all three middle schools. That sole category was maintaining confidentiality. In this sense, trust implied support.

In all three schools, teachers expressed feelings of being trusted and valued by their principals. Principals echoed having confidence in their staffs and in the professionalism of their teachers. Tony, the principal of Handy Middle School, posited, "This is how I deal with my staff and you're not going to see me looking over your shoulder at every moment to see what's going on in your room. You will be on your own to be a professional. I hired you as a professional, you are a professional." Sharing decisions and being collegial, he thought, demonstrated consistency and inspired confidence and trust between himself and his teachers.

In these three schools, there were some basic principles of trust, with local variation. Two principals claimed that trust meant having the same beliefs. Principals and teachers in two schools agreed that trust meant honesty or authenticity. In the third school, principals and teachers agreed that trust meant being an empathic listener. In all three schools, teachers concurred on one dimension of the meaning of trust: maintaining confidentiality. The teachers were a little clearer than the principals on what interpersonal trust meant to them because they shared more dimensions of trust in common.

3

TRUST-PROMOTING
LEADER BEHAVIORS

While listening to teachers and principals describe their perceptions of the meaning of trust, my mind wandered as to what precisely a principal could do to engender trust with the teaching staff. At each of the three schools I visited, principals and teachers had their own ideas about what particular behaviors of the principal promoted interpersonal trust. As I found with the meaning of trust, many of the behaviors of the principal that fostered trust depended on the school setting.

One particular leader behavior that engendered trust did stand out: building and sustaining relationships with teachers through various communicative and supportive behaviors of the principal. Let's examine specific communicative behaviors of the principal at each of the three schools.

COMMUNICATIVE BEHAVIORS
AT CHEERFUL MIDDLE SCHOOL

From the Principal's Perspective

Brad told me that, "You can't communicate enough about everything because it is in poor communication of what is really taking place that trust breaks down. People begin to make their own interpretations and interpretations can result in the loss of respect and trust for what the principal is really about." "Frequent communication," he emphasized, "is the antidote for so much of the mistrust that takes place between principal and teachers. It is important to let people know what is taking place, to keep people adequately informed about what our goals are, what is the progress of where we are, what is the plan. . . . Good communication probably has to do with the communication being accurate about the facts, letting communication be timely, that is close to the events, in a way that it gives good information to people to make other choices, decisions about the information."

"I believe in accurate communication with my teaching staff. This is my way of getting the teachers to trust me," Brad concluded. "In the past, I sent out paper memos to the entire faculty and the memos only were intended for a few teachers. These were disciplinary memos or were directives and were sometimes misinterpreted by teachers," he explained. Brad stressed "frequent, good, accurate communication" as a major trust-building behavior

One of the preferred modalities of communication for Brad was through electronics. When Brad first instituted technology in his school, it was awhile before most teachers felt comfortable using the software. Brad explained that he eased teachers into it, but continued to meet in-person with teachers whenever necessary. Brad now sends biweekly newsletters to parents and school personnel electronically, "I am the only principal in this school system who sends my newsletter by electronic mail . . . and I am most proud that I have developed an address book within the school for daily communications. . . . We do our business on e-mail every day and when our server is down, it gets people stressed out because we have taken away how we communicate with each other." This method, he suggested, allowed for the dissemination of timely, accurate communication. When the server was down, it created havoc because daily communication at Cheerful revolved around the interchange of information.

"Technology is a useful communication tool," Brad said. " I'm not comfortable with a paper memo because I end up whacking people that I don't want to whack. The electronic communication is working well for me because it allows me to write my memo to the people I really want to address. It could be addressed to small groups, it could be addressed to seventh grade teachers, it could be to math teachers, it could be to my department advisors. I can focus the group and then write in a less formal method." Technology allowed Brad to target his audience.

In spite of the success of electronic communication, Brad admitted that a face-to-face conversation with an individual teacher was the best mode of communication. "If it is necessary to have frequent conversations," Brad pointed out, "you don't catch all the players you need to get to. . . . That's why some principals and managers rely strictly on memos, so they can say they told everybody and that's the way it is." In remembering his entry plan, Brad recounted, "When I first came into this school I interviewed every staff member. It took two and a half months to do. I spent approximately forty-five minutes with every single member here. So that was part of my process of trying to learn about the staff and find out who key players are." Brad acknowledged the limitations of such individualized and time-consuming conversations.

In lieu of face-to-face conversations with teachers, Brad adhered to an open door policy. This allowed him to be a confidante to the teachers so that "when they want to talk to you about any issue, you are accepting . . . and they know that when they go to you, the trust is between you and them and whatever is said is said in confidence." Brad also expressed the importance of being visible throughout the building so that the teachers "can see you doing what you said you believe in and being available to them to seek you out for help as a resource."

Saving what he deemed the important trust-building behavior for last, Brad identified confronting conflict as a behavior that builds trust. Brad claimed that conflicts often arise between parents and teachers, students and teachers, and secretary and secretary. He felt that teachers see him as someone who seeks resolution to problems. He said he often hears the words, "I've got a problem. Can you help me?" He then added, "As a middle manager, I'm in the middle of conflict every day. . . . I'm always in the middle of trying to seek resolutions to problems." For Brad, conflict management was important in trust building.

In emphasizing the fragility of trust, Brad told me that "trust can be lost overnight. It is something that is vulnerable. You could have one event take place in a school and overnight a person or a group of teachers could lose trust because they thought things were one way and then things change the other way. . . . They may have a perception that things changed." Brad implied that misperception could cause conflict.

From the Teachers' Perspective

"I find our principal is very willing to listen and he appreciates it if you come up with different scenarios to present to him on any given topic," Cheerful teachers told me. These teachers described their principal as a person who admitted he did not have all the answers and that he talked freely with them to understand their positions on certain issues. They identified maintaining open and honest dialogue, being a good listener, and confronting any situation as practices that built trust between themselves and their principal.

Cheerful teachers underscored the value of having a principal who confronted conflicts. They emphasized, "A behavior that is least conducive to building trust is the reluctance to address issues or shifting the responsibility for the issue to somebody else." They expressed this notion in their response to a question about defining a barrier to trust.

COMMUNICATIVE BEHAVIORS AT HANDY MIDDLE SCHOOL

From the Principal's Perspective

"One of the strengths I brought to this school is a lot of informal dialogue with people about school issues," Tony told me. "Sometimes the dialogue takes place in the hall or the lunchroom or wherever we are," Tony explained.

"One of the things I do with teachers . . . is talk about the challenges of the administration, the kind of day-to-day things that we face as principals because teachers don't see them and so I want them to know we're working hard for them. . . . I believe, though I've never read anything about this, to be honest with you, but I believe the more they understand administration, and I know this for a fact, they say, I don't ever want to do what you do. And I think there is a lot of respect and trust for the job as principal." Tony worked hard to clarify and communicate his role as principal.

Although Tony fostered relationships based on one-to-one conversations of open, honest dialogue with his teachers, Tony mentioned that sometimes his faculty took their frustrations out on him. In the privacy of Tony's office, teachers were very blunt with him. Tony confronted these conflicts head-on.

"There are times when I've had to say to individual teachers," Tony recalled, "you've gone too far. I think this year, in particular, some of the frustrations are around some of the hygienic factors here, the building addition and renovations. People got a little bit too critical in the wrong settings and one-on-one in this office. I've said don't do that to me. I'm going to deal with that. But I think that dialogue, in a way, builds some trust, too, because it creates some parameters of relationship so that people know what's acceptable and what's not acceptable in terms of adult role. I think some teachers understand the dilemmas principals face with limited resources or sometimes difficult decisions." During the current renovation process, teachers went into Tony's office to complain about air quality, electrical issues, and other things that did not seem to go according to schedule.

Tony mentioned that he worked on consensus development with his teaching staff. Citing an example, he said, "We're going to come to some consensus, but in that consensus you change and that's been done on a small group basis as well as a large group basis. I remind people from time to time, even though they don't like it, they do work in an organization, they're not autonomous and that once there is a consensus we're going to move on and people have a professional obligation to grab hold of those goals and objectives." By bringing teachers to consensus, Tony felt the process promoted collegiality, open, honest communication, and an opportunity to explain a rationale for decision making. Tony insisted on the idea of consensus because his predecessor did not work that way with teachers. He claimed the process of developing consensus formed a platform for faculty trust building.

Along these lines, Tony shared his process of decision making with me. He told me, "I think when you spend time with the people to explain the rationale, to show them some of the dilemmas you face and explaining why you did what you did builds a little more trust." He acknowledged that this type of governance opened up the trust-building atmosphere with teachers and augmented a spirit of collaboration for consensus development.

Regarding the use of telecommunication, Tony mentioned, "We are not networked into the classrooms from the office. Even if we were, I think I would be a little reluctant in that, as principals, we've heard that cliché and warning, better say it than write it. And inevitably, whether it's a memo or e-mail, people are going to misunderstand that lack of interpersonal relationships and I don't think that's ultraconservative. . . . Another thing I do around trust is out of respect for teachers, I need to get the information they need without having a meeting because they're all busy and they want to focus on teaching. So I will do, by tongue and cheek, one of my morale-busting memos. I often do it right after vacation when I come in on Monday. Its cutesy and it's got little artsy stuff from the computer, but it's photocopied. I call it my morale-busting memo because inevitably, no matter how off beat it is, somebody says, 'this is awful . . . I can't win here.' I'm trying to keep you informed. I didn't want to have a meeting, but inevitably something gets hot because of the written words so every time I write and get that reaction, I'm reminded it's better to say it, better to have conversations and play things out on people than write it." In keeping with his feelings about relating to teachers in-person, preferably on a one-to-one basis, Tony reiterated his thoughts about the use of technology as a mode of communication.

From the Teachers' Perspective

"There are no hidden agendas in this building, there really aren't," bragged one of the Handy Middle School teachers. "That's right. Our principal has a collegial approach, involving his staff in everything that this building does. And he genuinely likes to model that," another Handy teacher claimed. "Well, I think it's the collegiality. It's a matter of sitting down and presenting the problem, as our principal does, putting the problem on the table and asking: What can we do about it? What are your ideas? What are your suggestions?" a third teacher posited. She continued, "There appear to be very few policies here and as a result, I think that trust is assumed because you don't have to worry am I meeting this directive or that directive. So there is not much policy written. It is a very open atmosphere."

These teachers knew that Tony prided himself on keeping them informed. The teachers told me that Tony's efforts to apprise them about the running of the school was an important trust-building behavior of their principal as was his ability to put things on the table for discussion.

One of the teachers remarked, "Some of us have been together so long that we have no difficulty going into and out of conflicts with one another or for that matter, with our principal. But conflicts get resolved here, for the most part. And I think the fact that conflict can surface safely and be dealt with and put to rest is a very important piece of trust building because if it couldn't be, then you couldn't trust his reactions to conflict or one another, for that matter. Conflict avoidance leads to a lack of trust because if everything gets shoved under the rug or something, then, at some point it is going to rise up and bite everybody." So these teachers identified the ability of their principal to resolve conflicts as a trust-building behavior.

COMMUNICATIVE BEHAVIORS AT WESTERN MIDDLE SCHOOL

From the Principal's Perspective

"Good listening requires a reaction. When somebody tells you something you have to react. If somebody comes looking for help or if somebody comes with a problem, what do I do about this, if you don't do something you haven't listened. I respond to teachers' concerns, and that's a big one," commented Nathan, the principal of Western Middle School. It seemed to Nathan that listening and responding to teachers contributed greatly to the trust-building process.

Although Nathan reported that he was an active listener, he did not fully embrace the concept of shared decision making, which involved listening to other peoples' voices. He claimed, "I'll listen to you beforehand, but I'm going to make the decision." When probed about his decision-making process, Nathan replied, "Well, I think there are all sorts of different decisions. There are some things that are adaptable to making group decisions and some things where people come in and say we've got this situation now and what are we going to do. . . . And for every decision you make some people are happy and some people are unhappy, and I think in terms of trust, you have to say to yourself do people trust, at least whether they like the decision to see if the motivation was correct because there are always going to be people who don't like the decision. A lot of times there are situations where you'll sit down and talk things over and a lot of times not." This notion of decision making implied that sometimes there would be conflicts with teachers about the decisions, but Nathan would listen to the teachers so that they felt they had been heard.

Nathan recalled two situations wherein he had confronted a teacher and told her directly that he would listen to her, but he would make the decision himself and another in which a teacher told him that he seemed to always get his way. These interchanges, according to Nathan, indicated that the communication between himself and his teachers was open and honest. They could confront conflict together by talking it out. Nathan recounted what he said to the teacher, "If I'm going to take the grief then I'm going to make the decision." In another instance, a teacher said to him, "I get the impression you expect to get your way all the time." Nathan responded, "That hurts. What are you telling me? Am I that rigid?" "No," she answered, "but I'm just telling you that's my take."

After reflection, when summarizing this principal–teacher dialogue, Nathan thought that if he listened to teachers and offered a rationale for his decisions, he could make certain decisions unilaterally. By listening to teachers and allowing them to express their feelings about him in open and honest dialogue, Nathan hinted that these practices were conducive to building trust between himself and his teachers and to diminishing conflicts. Nathan also mentioned that he occasionally writes a note to teachers, acknowledging some of their good work. He wondered if that recognition of their professionalism mattered in the trust-building process.

From the Teachers' Perspective

Western Middle School teachers felt that their principal opened his office door and listened to them. They felt that this "listening policy" was valuable for sustaining a trusting relationship between themselves and Nathan. One of them remarked, "I know there is a relationship of trust because I can go to him with just about any problem." Another added, "I know I can go to him at any time on any situation." These teachers stressed the importance of Nathan being available to them so that when they wanted to confront him with an issue, they could count on him to listen. They reported, "You can express an opinion that he does not support and sometimes you might sway him to your point of view. But many times you may not, and after you have disagreed, you can agree to disagree and there isn't any repercussion afterward or there isn't any baggage about it. It is just two points of view about this and we don't share the same one and that is fine. I think that is also a sign of a trusting relationship, but also a professional and respectful one."

Day-to-day interaction with Nathan was important to the teachers because they claimed that a real barrier to trust for them would be if the principal did not have daily contact or what they termed "regular contact" with the teachers. They boasted, "We have that and we like that." One of the reasons teachers decided that this frequent interaction was valuable in the trust-building process was their desire to be kept informed by Nathan about school happenings. "We like to be kept informed of what is going on, what the initiatives are that we are working on." As a corollary to this idea, teachers remarked that one of Nathan's practices, which they felt conductive to building trust, was that he scheduled frequent meetings. "Right now, meetings are frequent enough but before, I think last year or the year before, we probably didn't think so, we didn't have as many. We also think he is trying to reach out and get things on the agenda for the meetings, things that we want to see addressed. I think he, himself, realized that he needs to address certain things to reach the problems and concerns we have as teachers. We think he does a good job at listening." Nathan's practices of confronting conflict and listening served as communicative types of trust-building behaviors.

SUPPORTIVE BEHAVIORS AT CHEERFUL MIDDLE SCHOOL

From the Principal's Perspective

Brad told me that "one of the things I do is to try to build trust to support teachers in what they are doing by helping them, to go the extra mile for them, to make sure they have the resources." In the role he defined as "facilitator to the learning process," he explained, "that means to provide teachers with resources they need: training, time, schedule, materials, tools, all those things."

To Brad, support as a trust-building behavior meant more than supporting teachers' professionalism. It meant supporting teachers' personal lives, being a confidante, and recognizing their good work. "I support them in all the needs they have, to be a confidante to them when they want to talk to me about whatever issue and it might be an issue outside of school, it might be they are having a change in their lives and they need a person to rely on, so it's important that they have a person they can trust, a go-to person. I guess the other part is if things are going well, that they can feel okay and that they look at you as a person who will help them send out the good news that things are going well and that you are sharing their good news."

"I believe in basic trust in all staff and I start with that concept," Brad declared in response to my question about what policies he had in place to promote trust between himself and his teaching staff. Brad reiterated the value of his intuition in interpreting which teachers displayed a trusting attitude toward him. Brad's focus on maintaining a positive attitude toward the professionalism of teachers was one of his methods of fostering interpersonal trust.

What seemed like an important trust-building behavior to Brad was showing teachers that he worked hard. Brad felt that if his teaching staff saw him do the things he talked about, this type of authentic behavior promoted trust between himself and his teaching staff. "But if I talk about school improvement with the School Improvement Council, then you'd find me on a Saturday all day, with my hands dirty, digging holes and planting shrubs and trees, not just wishing we had a prettier school. Then they see me walking some of the talk." Brad felt that his hard work supported the hard work of teachers.

From the Teachers' Perspective

Cheerful teachers commented that having a principal like Brad, who was easy to talk to, was important in building trust. "He is down to earth, has a pleasant personality, and is sociable," one teacher noted. Another teacher acknowledged Brad's "open door policy." She said, "I don't feel I have to make an appointment. I feel like I can stop in the hall, stop downstairs, and the door is always open. It's a working give and take and that is important to me."

The principal's approach or attitude toward teachers seemed to be important in building faculty trust. Teachers spoke of having been in a school climate that was, prior to Brad's tenure, negative and that fostered a "negative approach to working with faculty." Teachers claimed that "as a unit, trust builds support with the faculty."

Along with maintaining a positive attitude toward the teaching staff, Cheerful teachers felt that the principal needed to be fair. They stated that sometimes principals may have preconceived opinions of teachers and that kind of attitude does not promote trust. Principals, they acknowledged, needed to be flexible and change their opinions if new facts are presented. They needed to be open-minded and flexible. Speaking in general terms, these teachers said that the principal needed to "go back to a situation, reevaluate, and listen." The teachers told me that an "empathic" principal would be able to do this and that this type of behavior would be trust building.

Cheerful teachers identified some particularly supportive practices of their principal that promoted trust between themselves and Brad: showing empathy and having a flexible attitude. In addition, the teachers suggested that their principal's vulnerability engendered trust. Several of them mentioned, "It has been my experience that this principal is able to admit he is wrong and, in this building, he has revisited his opinion about certain teachers and reassessed them in a positive way and I respect him for that. I think if a principal is narrow-minded and can't admit that he can ever be wrong and that somebody else might have a better point of view or that you've actually made a mistake, then that is a behavior that will break down trust."

One of the teachers told me that Brad "admits he is a generalist and that he has to wear many hats during the course of the day and that he relies on our expertise in certain areas depending on our position. He is willing to come forward and be proactive in many instances and admit when something is wrong and he asks us for our opinion, professional and personal."

All of these teachers stressed the importance of the principal behaving in a manner that maintained confidentiality. They explained that if they confided in the principal, they would not want to find out later that their confidence had been betrayed. A collegial style of leadership seemed important to them in fostering interpersonal trust. "I feel that our principal is supportive of the action we take on certain issues and I feel comfortable going to him."

Teachers stated that their principal recognized their professionalism and respected them by seeking their opinions when he was not knowledgeable about something. "I appreciate it very much when he asks the opinion of others who are specialists in the field, that he trusts the opinions of people who are experts in that field and will fully back that position because he trusts his staff." This was mentioned again by another teacher's comment, "Our principal is interested in us as teachers and makes efforts to come into our classrooms."

In addition to Brad knowing the teachers professionally, Cheerful teachers pointed out the importance of their principal's display of care and concern for them. This type of caring behavior helped foster trust, they claimed, by creating a supportive school climate. "I also think it is important that the principal realizes that you have a life and family beyond school and we happen to have a principal like that here," a teacher commented. "If a family situation occurs, there's a lot of support to address that family situation, whether it's a health issue or an educational issue or whatever. It's real important to the person in the building to know that if something came up that you'd have the support to take care of the things you need to and that has been very helpful to me." Adding that, "Brad takes the time to look at everything you bring to the table and responds and does something in a caring and meaningful way," another teacher acknowledged the value of this type of trust-building behavior.

Cheerful teachers indicated that Brad tried to be flexible and fair in his opinions and was responsive to their needs. All of these practices fostered trust in their relationship with their principal. During our conversation, these teachers referred to Brad as being responsive and following through on what he said he would do. They said, "Response time is generally good with our principal and his door is always open." I concluded that at Cheerful, the major trust-building behaviors and practices centered around building and sustaining principal–teacher relationships. The behaviors of the principal that fostered relationship building were communicating with teachers and supporting them.

SUPPORTIVE BEHAVIORS
AT HANDY MIDDLE SCHOOL

From the Principal's Perspective

In my conversation with Tony, he focused on efforts to encourage feedback and honesty from his teachers. "I develop that early on," Tony claimed. He continued, "By soliciting feedback from staff, I am showing support for my teaching staff by recognizing them as equals."

Recognizing the good work that teachers do was a trust-building behavior that Tony identified. He pointed out that his collegial leadership style indicated that a certain amount of trust was being built. He provided the following evidence, "I think another thing that I do which builds trust is to get into the classroom. I don't criticize the teachers, but I write little notes about how nice the class was today. Also, when I see some great teaching going on, I highlight some of that, either verbally or in writing."

Tony explained that the principal who had preceded him at Handy Middle School was a "military officer and believed in administration similar to an autocratic style." Tony felt that over a period of time Handy teachers became used to his new, collegial style of leadership and that the teachers now felt respected. Tony said that from the first day of his tenure, he informed teachers of his preference to work collaboratively. As evidence of his collaboration with teachers, Tony mentioned that he and his teachers wrote a mission statement and a handbook. They also discussed the drug and alcohol problems that were present when he began his tenure in 1993.

Tony referenced his daily visits to classrooms and corridors. He said that by being in classes, teachers had access to him and could ask him questions and remind him about something he may have forgotten to do or they could dialogue with him about anything on their minds, without waiting for an appointment. By wandering the corridors, informal dialogues occurred. Tony proudly stated, "Teachers are comfortable with me being in their classes while they are teaching. They're very aware that I am around the building all day and so there are no symbolic blocks to any communication because I'm around most of the time. . . . You see, by being visible, I am supportive."

"I go into an eighth grade class on students' rights," Tony continued, "so that teachers can see me teach. I think the ultimate trust in this business is that teachers know their principals are teachers first and they can teach and really empathize and can talk the teacher talk. I can talk the same language as the teachers and show I understand their work. I think the other thing you would hear about trust . . . is that I know my students." Connecting with students, Tony said, showed his teaching staff that he, like them, is a teacher, which demonstrated trust.

From the Teachers' Perspective

"I think he takes a collegial approach most of the time," one Handy teacher explained. "He sets common goals, comes up with common resolutions, and involves the staff as much as possible in the decision-making process. I think this really helps in the building of trust," she clarified.

"That's right," verified another teacher. "He does not have issues of power and control," quipped another teacher. The teachers agreed that a spirit of collegiality prevailed at Handy. Teachers postulated that by putting things on the table and asking for their input, as well as by demonstrating support and respect for their work, Tony increased the trust between himself and them.

One of the teachers, who also was the building union representative, discussed a situation that demonstrated this type of collegial and supportive behavior of her principal. She spelled out an instance where "Tony filled me in on a situation where he had taken a very hard-line stand on a case in this building and later realized that he should not have been that hard-lined, but he did make it very clear to me up front that there would be times when we might not agree and that was going to be okay and that he could take a hard-line, but he would also be respectful of where I was and I should feel the same way with him. He said it was not a personal issue." Tony communicated that the teachers are professionals and are respected as such.

When asked what they might consider a barrier to trust, these teachers named a lack of availability. "If principals are not there when you need them, then you don't have much of a way to build trust, if they really tend to lock themselves behind their door." This was not the case with Tony, since he described himself as a visible principal. One of the teachers said she enjoyed her principal's visits to her class. Sharing her exuberance at his visits, she exclaimed, "I love it, I'm thrilled. I'm like, you want to see what we're doing, let me show you. I'm so excited to see administrators and people come though my classroom." Another teacher told me that Tony came frequently to her class and that was important because by visiting classes, their principal could understand what they were doing.

Teachers expressed that their principal's ability to follow through and show his vulnerability were behaviors that engendered trust. "Quite honestly, I think a principal who follows through is one who creates a trusting relationship. Our principal tells us he is not a detail person, so we bother him, but he lets us and this admission of his weakness and allowing us to bother him is a way for him to follow through," one teacher explained. Another teacher volunteered that "she never caught him in the act of not being trusting. Our former principal said things and did not follow up on them. This principal tells us to remind him to follow up. A third teacher commented that Tony "walked the talk and talked the talk." He was who he said he was.

These teachers acknowledged Tony's respect for their personal and professional lives, his trust in those whom he hired, and his confidence in the teachers. Teachers said that by seeking their input on issues, Tony demonstrated trust

SUPPORTIVE BEHAVIORS
AT WESTERN MIDDLE SCHOOL

From the Principal's Perspective

Nathan said he had been in the same school system for twenty-nine years, which enabled him to build a solid reputation. "People are familiar with me, they knew of me when I came here. They haven't found many surprises and I think that's an element of the trust factor, too. They pretty much know where you're coming from and they know how you're going to deal with things. They're not surprised by a reaction that might come out of left field. . . . I think the most important behavior is consistency." Nathan thought that his follow-through showed teachers he was trustworthy. "It is important to show teachers that I do something I said I was going to do, that's a biggie." My conversation with Nathan led me to believe that his regimen of consistent, reliable behavior promoted faculty trust.

Nathan seemed proud to talk about being available to his teaching staff. He indicated that this was a supportive trust-building behavior that encouraged relationship building between himself and his teachers. Nathan bragged to me that seven mornings a week he could be found in a local coffee shop. He said that teachers and parents alike knew where he was and at what time, so they could always contact him. He said that by making himself available, teachers could count and rely on him. Nathan boasted, "Teachers call me there at six in the morning. . . . They may have a family emergency but they know where to find me."

Personal support for teachers echoed throughout my conversation with Western's principal. Nathan cited a time when his superintendent had called him about a teacher who was taking a personal day before a long weekend. The superintendent said that Nathan should not have authorized the leave. Nathan urged the superintendent to check that teacher's attendance record and then to call him back. He told her that particular teacher needed out-patient surgery and that was the only day possible for scheduling the surgery. Nathan reported that his school does not have a high teacher-absentee rate and he felt that was indicative of the way in which he behaved toward teachers, displaying care and concern for them as people. "I think it all comes down to treating them like you understand what they're going through at whatever particular moment. What's going on in their lives is just as important as what's going on in the lives of the kids sitting in front of them. If both of them aren't the way they should be, then it isn't going to work."

"Acknowledging empathy for teachers is integral to the trust-building process," Nathan said. "At the same time, working with a staff of people who are at different stages . . . allows you to have some empathy for what they are going through." Nathan offered a vivid example of such empathic support for teachers' personal lives. "A lot of times people will come in and they'll ask for things that they know they probably shouldn't get and I'll say to them, 'If you don't take care of your own family first, what are you going to do with somebody else's kids?'"

Nathan then referred to a teacher who had come in that very morning of our conversation. Her narrative of what had happened to her the week before provided a vivid example of empathic behavior. Nathan recounted, "She had some difficulties last week and I just walked into her classroom one day and she came back and said 'What do I do?' I said, 'Nothing. It's over. It's done with. Go home and take care of it. I'll take care of the class. I can do double duty. I can still do eighth grade math.' You have to be able to empathize with what teachers are going through. They all have issues. They all have their own kids. They all have elderly parents. They all have husbands or wives. . . . You have to treat people as human beings."

Nathan described the time he puts into his job. Living close by, he sometimes comes back to school at night and on weekends. "I think time investment often equates to trust, too. You know, people might say: 'Does he care about what's going on if he's not willing to put in the time?' Also, by staying late and coming in on a Saturday to get organized allows me more time to be with teachers and to get caught up on paperwork." Nathan was proud of the fact that he lived in the same town as where Western was located and had built a fine reputation in the town. He delighted in saying that he occasionally jogged by the school and if teachers or parents were around there or in the community, they could talk to him about anything. "Trust may be a question of reputation. I managed to build mine up over the years being in the school system." Nathan postulated that by letting teachers and parents see him work hard, his dedication is a component of building trust between himself and his teaching staff.

From the Teachers' Perspective

"Our principal apologizes. He has a human side," Western Middle School teachers admitted. "We see him working hard. . . . He is here at night, going to meetings, and we know he has an interest in this particular building, in us as teachers, and in the students that are here. Our principal has given us that feeling of confidence and that feeling of trust." Another teacher offered that she could go to Nathan about anything and he "would not hold it against her," and moreover, he would keep her confidence. These teachers referred to Nathan as a real human being who is not perfect, but is someone who works hard for the good of the school. They recognized their principal as an honest person who was consistent in his behavior and did not portray favoritism or bias toward individual teachers.

These teachers expressed their feelings about trust-building behaviors in relation to attitude. They claimed, "It's a positive attitude, as opposed to a negative attitude wherein someone looks for bad things, that builds this feeling of trust." The Western teachers talked about being fearful of a principal who might, what they termed, "spy" on them and look over their shoulders to see how they were doing. They did not point their finger at Nathan, but emphasized how strongly they looked to him to be nonjudgmental and open-minded.

This idea was substantiated by one teacher's description of a hypothetical incident wherein a student might be sent to Nathan and the student might complain about the teacher. The teachers felt that Nathan would come back to them and ask them about the situation. They suspected he would say, "Tell me what happened," rather than coming back to them with a threatening attitude and saying, "Why did you throw this kid out or what did you do to this kid?" Or "Why didn't you look over his test paper?" as opposed to what they thought was displaying "a threatening attitude," he might simply ask, "What happened?" Or he might offer a positive suggestion.

At this school, teachers made clear what they considered supportive behavior of the principal, behavior that they felt led to trust building between the principal and themselves. They defined supportive behavior as that which demonstrates that "the principal is caring, that he knows us, he knows us outside of school, he knows us as people. . . . He acts in our best interests, the best interests of the kids, the best interests of the parents and the school. . . . He understands our goals. . . . He is supportive to programs. . . . He allows us to participate in any activities that allow us to continue our professional development above and beyond what's offered within the school system and the fact that he knows us as individual persons and he trusts us as professionals . . . allows us to go the extra mile of getting to know each other as people." One teacher offered, "Our principal is big enough professionally to allow other people to shine so that shows that we can trust him." Public acclaim of the teachers' good work also indicated supportive principal behavior because it showed the teachers that their principal recognized their professionalism.

Teachers found that when Nathan offered constructive criticism and suggested another way to handle a tough situation, this type of behavior was helpful and supportive. They pointed to the occasional notes of acknowledgment they received from their principal as demonstrations of his recognition, respect, and care for them as people and as professionals. All of these indicators of teacher support meant a great deal in the trust-building process at Western Middle School. "Our principal," they declared, "does not question your motives when you ask for something, suggest something, or make an attempt that you're working for the best interests of the students, parents, school."

These teachers explained that the school committee and the superintendent did not recognize their professionalism. Therefore, recognition from their principal meant a lot to them; he trusted them.

In the next chapter, I look more closely at what practitioners are saying about trust and about how to promote it.

4

MAKING SENSE OF
PRINCIPAL–TEACHER
PERCEPTIONS OF TRUST

Table 1 summarizes what practitioners said about the meaning of trust in schools. The bold text reflects some commonalities in their responses. This table indicates that principals and teachers did not share the exact same definitions of trust. Principals identified several dimensions of trust in common. They perceived interpersonal trust as their ability to do what they say, to be honest, and to have the same beliefs as their teaching staffs. Teachers agreed with principals in describing honesty as an element of interpersonal trust, and they added a new dimension: maintaining confidentiality.

Perceptions of the meaning of trust varied and were contingent on the setting. Trust often called for a description of actions to be carried out by the principal. Principals and teachers spoke of trust in terms of actions because they needed to see, feel, or do something tangible in order for trust to have meaning for them.

Conversations with both teachers and principals specifically revealed the following about the meaning of trust:

1. Teachers in all three schools said that trust meant maintaining confidentiality.
2. Principals in all three schools alluded to their own authenticity or honesty as a dimension of trust.

Table 1. The Meaning of Trust in Three Schools

School	Cheerful	Handy	Western
Principal	1. **walk the talk** 2. **honesty** 3. **having same beliefs** 4. belief in basic trust of teachers 5. positive attitude and intuition	1. **walk the talk** 2. **honesty** 3. follow-through 4. admitting when you don't know 5. developing and sustaining relationships with teachers 6. informal dialogue	1. **teachers haven't found surprises with me** 2. **open, free dialogue** 3. **having the same beliefs** 4. being an active listener 5. people have faith to come to me with problems 6. being empathic
Teachers	1. **mutual honesty** 2. **confidentiality** 3. **recognition of teachers** 4. fairness 5. respect 6. follow-through 7. mutual involvement	1. **honest** and open 2. **confiding in our principal** 3. **communication of expectations** 4. **show confidence in teachers** 5. show vulnerability 6. intuition/feeling of being trusted	1. **having principal give us information we need** 2. **confiding in our principal** 3. being empathic 4. having principal listen to us

3. Principals and teachers in all three schools agreed on at least one element of the meaning of trust within their own school. In Cheerful Middle School, the element was authenticity, in Handy, it was authenticity and communication, and in Western, it was reliability and communication.

Although the meaning of trust varied according to the school setting, all three principals believed that an underlying dimension of the meaning of trust was in the one-to-one relationships they were sustaining with their teaching staffs. Interpersonal trust involved the principals demonstrating reliability, consistency, and follow-through.

In each school, principals and teachers explained trust in terms of what was happening within their own school settings. Let's look at perceptions of the meaning of trust in these three schools.

PERCEPTIONS OF THE MEANING OF TRUST

Reliability

Nathan, the Western Middle School principal, and his teachers suggested that one of the aspects of the meaning of trust was reliability. In clarifying, Nathan said, "Teachers haven't found many surprises with me and I think that's probably an element of the trust factor. They pretty much know where I am coming from." Given Nathan's twenty-nine-year tenure in the Western school, reliability meant providing a sense of constancy or "staying the course."

Another meaning of trust in Western Middle School, as perceived by one teacher, was the dimension of trust as reliability. In speaking about interpersonal trust, the teacher mentioned her principal and said, "I think that having this consistency or longevity with him is important, knowing things don't change."

In this particular school, teachers told me that neither the school committee nor the superintendent respected them. Consequently, they did not feel secure in their positions. I suspect that this insecurity necessitated reliance on their principal being there when it counts, by supporting them.

Reliability as an aspect of trust did not play as integral a part in the principals' and teachers' perceptions of trust at Cheerful and Handy as it did at Western. Principals and teachers from these two newly renovated, suburban middle schools focused on describing interpersonal trust in terms of being honest, being real or authentic, and being intuitive and positive about one another. Having more resources meant having more job security, which impacted the meaning of interpersonal trust.

What I found out by talking with teachers from both Handy and Cheerful Middle Schools was that these teachers, unlike those with whom I met at Western, were teacher leaders. They were department heads, team leaders, union representatives, or they held national teacher board certification. These teachers felt respected and secure in their jobs. Therefore, they did not require as much support from their principals as did the teachers in Western Middle School. This positive feeling influenced their perceptions of trust.

Handy teachers commented, "If I would say anything about trust it's an intuitive thing, we simply do not have the sense that someone is watching all the time." Handy teachers experienced autonomy, in that Tony did not hover over them. I found the same notion expressed by Brad and his teachers at Cheerful.

Consistency and Follow-Through

Consistency and follow-through were aspects of the substance of interpersonal trust in all three schools. The principals' actions played a role in the meaning of trust in all three schools. At Western, Nathan emphasized empathic, active listening as part of the meaning of interpersonal trust. He stated that he responded consistently to teachers whenever they asked him to listen to them, even listening to personal problems. Nathan knew that his teachers needed to rely on his consistent, active listening. He said that this promoted the confidence of his staff and that confidence was part of trust. Nathan's teachers commented, "I think trust is communicating with your principal. . . . I think being listened to is part of trust. Our principal does a good job trying to listen to all of us." Carrying out this idea of the principal relating to teachers, Nathan declared that trust was the faith of his teachers to come to him and tell him anything and he would listen to them with empathy. Trust, then, within the context of Western Middle School, was perceived as an action.

Another manifestation of consistency in Western was the long-time reputation of Nathan, their principal. Nathan boasted that he knew his community for almost twenty-nine years, because he had been a high school assistant principal in the same district prior to his tenure as Western Middle School principal. He claimed that he had built his reputation through longevity in the community, both as school leader and resident. Having been part of the community for so long, Nathan held the same beliefs as his teachers. He said that those common beliefs were part of the substance of trust.

Like Nathan, Cheerful's principal perceived trust as encouraging relationships with his teaching staff by sharing consistently the same beliefs and information. Part of the meaning of trust hinged on the principal being able to communicate with his teachers whenever necessary and demonstrating confidence and faith in the teaching staff. Cheerful teachers expressed content that their principal came to them when he was not sure of something, encouraging input from them.

Tony, the Handy Middle School principal, stressed the meaning of trust as building and sustaining relationships by being available to talk informally with his staff. Handy teachers agreed that consistent, informal dialogue served as a dimension of trust.

In all three schools, teachers expressed feelings of being trusted and valued by their principals. Principals echoed having confidence in their staffs and in the professionalism of their teachers.

PERCEPTIONS OF TRUST-BUILDING BEHAVIORS, PRACTICES, AND POLICIES

The principals and teachers with whom I met identified specific behaviors of the principal that engendered trust within their own school communities. Table 2 summarizes what these principals and teachers selected as the most trust-inspiring behaviors of the principal. This table shows that the most frequently voiced behaviors of the principal that fostered trust were confronting conflicts, showing vulnerability, and being available. The overarching trust-promoting behavior enumerated by all three principals was building and sustaining one-to-one relationships with teachers via communicative and supportive behaviors.

Principals and teachers in all three middle schools suggested that the principal needed to support teachers and communicate with them in order to build trusting relationships. These people said that the specific type of communicative or supportive practice varied according to what was going on in each school or what had been going on in each school prior to the tenure of the current principal.

From our conversations, it was apparent that the most frequently mentioned trust-building behavior of the principal was confronting conflict. Principals and teachers described the value of the principal being able to display open behavior by putting issues on the table for teachers to agree and disagree. In opening the lines of communication, principals claimed they were building and sustaining trusting relationships with their teaching staffs. Now let's look at how these principals addressed conflict and built one-to-one relationships.

Confronting Conflict

"As a middle manager, I'm in the middle of conflict every day. . . . I'm always in the middle of trying to seek resolutions to problem solving positions, so conflict management is important in trust building," Brad, the Cheerful principal, told me. Brad further explained that he often heard the words, "I've got a problem, can you help me?" He said that conflicts cropped up between parents and teachers, students and teachers, and secretary and secretary. Since he was the principal, Brad felt that he was viewed as the person to resolve conflicts. With his focus on communication, confronting conflict involved talking things out.

Western's principal, Nathan, recalled two situations wherein he had confronted some teachers and told them directly that he would listen to them, but that he would also make the decision himself. Nathan explained to one of the teachers, "If I'm going to take the grief, then I'm going to make the decision." The teachers involved conveyed displeasure with their principal's remark because they felt he "always got his way," but acknowledged that their voices were heard. Eager to build one-to-one relationships with his teaching staff, Nathan told me he was open and displayed vulnerability when conversing with teachers. He inquired of the teachers, "That hurts. What are you telling me? Am I that rigid?" Western teachers attributed their principal's open attitude and willingness to admit any mistakes as a trust-building behavior conducive to conflict resolution.

At the Handy Middle School, open dialogue, sometimes in the form of confronting conflict, anchored trust-building behaviors of the principal. With the renovation problem, Tony, Handy's principal, recounted,

Table 2. Most Commonly Identified Trust-Building Behaviors in Schools

Informants	Behaviors	Practices	Policies
Principal and Teachers Cheerful Middle School	1. confront conflicts 2. be visible 3. be available 4. work hard	1. show vulnerability 2. follow through 3. maintain confidence 4. respect teachers personally and professionally	
Principal and Teachers Handy Middle School	1. confront conflicts 2. be visible 3. be available	1. show vulnerability 2. lead collegially 3. keep teachers informed 4. show respect for teacher professionalism 5. keep open dialogue	
Principal and Teachers Western Middle School	1. confront conflicts by talking 2. be available 3. work hard 4. be consistent 5. be responsive	1. show vulnerability	1. write notes to acknowledge good work of teachers 2. have an active listening policy

"People got a little too critical in the wrong setting and on one-to-one in this office." He confronted these teachers and told them how he was going to deal with things. He felt that confronting conflict and talking with teachers in a face-to-face conversation was a more effective way to engender trust than by sending a memo. Tony stressed the need to clarify his role as middle manager to teachers so that his teaching staff could understand why certain things happened as they did in the building renovation process. Tony surmised that this open, informal dialogue avoided some potential conflict.

Building One-to-One Relationships

Of the three principals with whom I met, Tony identified the greatest number of behaviors and practices that engendered interpersonal trust in his school. Given the context of Handy Middle School, both before and after Tony's 1993 arrival, it was apparent that more guidelines needed to be set to train teachers to work collaboratively and to achieve consensus development.

When Tony began his tenure, he met one-to-one with teachers, explaining how he was going to solicit teacher input. His plan was to bring problems to the table for discussion. Tony explained that he was going to be visible throughout the school for informal dialogue. Since the preceding principal had not been accessible, veteran teachers were not used to Tony's collegial leadership style. Tony explained that over time, he sought teacher input on issues and taught teachers consensus development skills.

As Handy teachers put it, "Our principal puts problems on the table and asks how we can resolve them together." This was accomplished by Tony's ability to concentrate on consensus development by talking with teachers on a one-to-one basis. He also focused on being available and visible, providing timely, accurate information to teachers, showing vulnerability when he forgot or did not know something, asking for feedback and honesty from teachers, and recognizing good work.

One of the teachers with whom I spoke commented that when she arrived at Handy as a building transfer from the art department, Tony called her into his office for a one-to-one conference. At that time, he explained, "There would be times when we might not agree and that was going to be okay and that he could take a hard-line, but he would also be respectful of where I was and I should feel the same way with him.

He said it was not a personal issue. So he communicated that we are professionals and we are respected as such."

From my talk with Tony, it appeared that his collegial style of leadership and his focus on maintaining one-to-one relationships with teachers were critical in maintaining trust between himself and his teaching staff. Tony claimed that if he apprised teachers about what he could and could not do within the confines of his job, teachers would better ascertain his desire to work hard for them, and they would understand the limitations of his position. This kind of dialogue would keep the communication open, increasing the trust. Like Brad, Cheerful's principal, Tony sometimes needed to be reminded by his staff about following through. In this way, Tony concluded that he was promoting faculty trust by showing vulnerability and honesty.

Both Brad and Tony acknowledged individual, face-to-face conversations with teachers as an effective way to engender trust. Brad pointed out the difficulty in getting around the school to talk with each teacher. He emphasized, however, that he communicated to teachers what his expectations were for them and his own goals and beliefs, and followed through on what he said he would do. Brad claimed that these were his trust-building behaviors.

Similar to Tony, Brad refrained from writing memos. He explained that in the past, when he was a principal elsewhere, his paper memos had been misinterpreted. Since Cheerful Middle School had superb internal telecommunications, Brad communicated electronically, on a daily basis, with his teaching staff. Like Tony, Brad felt that having an open door policy, confronting conflict, being visible and available, following through, recognizing good work, and showing vulnerability were all trust-building behaviors.

Brad identified communication with as many individual teachers as possible as the most important trust-building behavior in his school. Having been a technology director, Brad felt that providing teachers with accurate, timely, and good information was a way of building trust and, at the same time, developing one-to-one relationships with teachers. When he began his tenure at Cheerful, Brad sought out what he thought were key players on his teaching staff. Based on individual conferences conducted with each teacher, Brad acquired information about the school.

One of the Cheerful teachers with whom I met mentioned that when Brad began his tenure two and a half years prior, the school climate was poor. Some teachers remarked that before Brad had become principal, there was a "negative approach to working with the faculty." One teacher suggested that some of the trust-building behaviors initiated by Brad included "being fair to all teachers, seeking input from everyone, keeping confidence, and being open-minded and flexible." Cheerful teachers underscored the value of feeling supported by Brad. This notion corroborated their principal's perception of trust-building behavior.

The teachers and principal at Western Middle School identified active listening as the most effective way to build trusting one-to-one relationships with teachers. Raving that their principal always listened to them, no matter what, Western Middle School teachers boasted that they could go to Nathan to vent about anything and that he would not hold that against them. They affirmed that their principal consistently responded to them, cared about them personally and professionally, and followed through, even if they needed to remind him. This was evident on the day I visited Western. A teacher came into Nathan's office to thank him for having covered her class when she was called home for an emergency.

Western teachers volunteered a portrait of their principal that characterized and summarized what they perceived as his supportive trust-building relationship behavior. Some of these behaviors may have been simpler for Nathan to put into effect than Brad and Tony because Nathan lived close to the school and had remained associated with the district for so long. Here is what Western teachers defined as supportive behavior of their principal, "Our principal demonstrates that he is caring, that he knows us outside of school, he knows us as people. . . . He acts in our best interests, the best interests of the kids, the best interests of the parents and the school. . . . He understands our goals. . . . He is supportive to programs. . . . He allows us to participate in any activities that allow us to continue our professional development above and beyond what's offered within the school system and the fact that he knows us as individual persons and he trusts us as professionals . . . allows us to go the extra mile of getting to know each other as people."

Testimonies from these teachers and principals suggest that principals, in addition to being instructional leaders, need to be strong enough to confront conflicts and have the interpersonal skills to listen to teachers, maintain their confidence, and encourage and motivate them by recognizing their professionalism and personal lives.

In chapter 5, I discuss what implications these behaviors have for current and aspiring principals, teachers, and other school leaders.

5

WHAT DOES ALL THIS MEAN FOR PRACTITIONERS?

An important discovery came from my talks with teachers. What I found out is that teachers who assumed leadership roles within their schools felt secure and respected. Their feelings of self-respect influenced their perceptions of trust. These teacher leaders did not require as much support from their principals. For them, reliability of the principal was a less important ingredient of trust. Consequently, fewer supportive leader behaviors seemed necessary to promote trust. Trust was implicit in these schools; manifest more as a positive attitude or an intuition of the principal and the teachers.

On the other hand, teachers who did not feel respected needed more tangible communicative and supportive behavior from their principal to demonstrate trust. I suspect there are many other teachers who feel similarly. Consequently, it is useful to have a handful of ways to promote it.

Based on feedback received from teachers and principals, I created a guide of leader behaviors conducive to engendering faculty trust. I call specific leader behaviors "trust enhancers." To make it easy to read the trust enhancer list, I've categorized the behaviors in table 3 as either supportive or communicative. The two most frequently mentioned leader behaviors, confronting conflict and maintaining confidence, appear in bold.

Table 3. Suggested Trust Enhancers for Principals

Supportive Behaviors	Communicative Behaviors
1. **Maintain confidentiality**	1. **Confront conflict** and try to resolve it
2. Treat all teachers fairly	2. Provide timely, accurate information
3. Be consistently responsive	3. Articulate goals and expectations
4. Demonstrate follow-through	4. Practice empathic, active listening
5. Solicit input from teachers	5. Be visible for informal dialogue
6. Praise and recognize good work	6. Maintain open door policy/availability
7. Be reliable	7. Plan meetings as necessary
8. Lead collegially	8. Share decision making
9. Respect teachers' opinions	
10. Be considerate and caring about teachers' personal lives	
11. Be respectful of teachers' professionalism	
12. Be willing to admit mistakes	

These actions, or leadership practices, are the essence of building one-to-one relationships between principals and teachers, the most necessary ingredient to promoting trust in schools.

IMPLICATIONS FOR PRACTICE

Trust is a leveraging tool. It is the foundation on which the principal can build and sustain one-to-one relationships with his or her teaching staff, especially when the principal is new to the school or when there are many new teachers in the school. Much of our initial behavior in new or stressful situations is an attempt to search for, test, and initiate a tentative sense of trust or mistrust. Recent interviews with new teachers suggest that among the reasons they are leaving the profession within five years of beginning their teaching is a lack of support from their administrators. Principals should be allowed time to build relationships before change is demanded. How else can they effect such types of trust enhancers as maintaining confidentiality and resolving conflicts?

J. Archer reports that the current New York City school chancellor is holding New York City schools more accountable by issuing "report cards" on principals. The performance evaluations on the system's principals focuses on student test-score gains and attendance. These are used in principals' job reviews. One criticism of these report cards states that "the reports fail to reflect the varying challenges that different schools face" (Archer, 2003, p. 4). The reports also fail to describe the principals' attempts to promote interpersonal trust, thereby impacting school improvement efforts. Teachers and principals need to be on the same team, all rooting to boost student achievement. It seems inappropriate to measure student test scores without knowing about the principal–teacher relationships. School improvement is contextual, contingent on how the school leader can rally his or her faculty to collaborate in raising student achievement.

Currently, there are public school principals who, as middle managers, have the responsibility for student achievement, but they do not have the authority. As middle managers, their hands are tied by their superintendents. Superintendents who hire principals need to trust that their principals can allocate their own instructional budgets for maximum student achievement. Without authority to allocate their own instructional budgets, principals will have difficulty improving schools. Teachers told me that the greatest barrier to ensuring faculty trust is the role of the principal as middle manager. They argue that principals should have site-based management, which includes school budget control.

In addition to having control of their school budgets, principals should be allowed to hire their own teachers, without superintendent approval. Principals and teachers know who will fit into their school cultures and who will be able to work well with them.

In some school districts, superintendents defer to principals for teacher hires and for building-based budgetary decisions. I have been in schools where this happens and have observed that the principal and teaching staff feel empowered. They feel trusted and respected and make their decisions collaboratively, building consensus as much as possible. Their decisions are based on the needs of their students. In these schools, an undercurrent of trust pervades corridors, classrooms, the library/media center, the cafeteria, and the teachers' lounge.

It is in this last place, the teachers' lounge, where the real culture of faculty trust is found. Teachers in these schools share their strategies for lesson design, expose their failed lesson plans, discuss exemplary practices, and pool resources to come up with better ideas for improving student academic performance. In this kind of school, a principal can step into the teachers' lounge and discussion continues.

THE PRINCIPAL HIRING PROCESS

The public school principal hiring process should be restructured to identify applicants skilled at promoting one-to-one relationships with teachers. This capability cannot be detected in many of the current processes of hiring principals. Having personally experienced the principal hiring procedure, I feel comfortable describing this process from my perspective.

Let's begin with the advertisement process. Advertisements for public school principals emphasize a master's degree in education, five years' experience in teaching, at least three years of administrative experience, and valid certification.

These advertisements do not require an applicant to possess such interpersonal skills as active listening, conflict resolution, or the ability to work collaboratively. Yet, among the reasons public school principal contracts are not renewed is the lack of these very same interpersonal skills.

In addition to the qualifications enumerated in advertisements, applications for public school principal positions have included essays on the following topics, "What is your vision for our school? What is your opinion of the zero tolerance policy? Write a statement of your philosophy of education." Here again, there is no opportunity for prospective public school principals to describe their relationship-building skills.

Usually, there are three or more interviews for the position of public school principal. First, there is the screening interview, wherein a ten- to fourteen-member search committee squeezes around one or two banquet-sized tables. The composition of the committee varies, but usually includes a principal from the district, an assistant superintendent, a few department heads, a special education director, a parent, a school board member, and occasionally a teacher. For a forty-five-minute period, each person, sometimes in succession around a table, asks a question from a list of predetermined questions.

Often, the opening question is, "Tell us about yourself." This is followed by some hypothetical scenario in which an applicant describes what he or she would do in such and such a case. Other questions may be: "What is your most significant achievement? How do you use student assessment data? How do you go about designing a curriculum?"

The group interview concludes with, "We only have a minute or so left, but is there anything you want us to ask that we did not cover in our questions?"

This first forty-five minute interview is the screening interview, a time for search committee members to decide whether they want to see the candidate again. If they do, candidates move to the semifinalist stage, at which time applicants' candidacies may be made public. During the semifinalist stage, a spontaneous writing sample is solicited, wherein a writing prompt is given and a candidate has twenty to thirty minutes to respond to a hypothetical situation, sometimes about discipline, budget constraints, or state curriculum standards. The sample is submitted in a sealed envelope to a personnel assistant. Applicants do not receive feedback on the writing sample. Usually, three semifinalists are selected, one of whom is often an internal candidate.

If a candidate survives the semifinalist stage, search committee members conduct a site visit of the now-finalist's current school. At that time, the finalist assembles some representative professional colleagues to talk with members of the search committee.

The last hurdles in this process are meetings with the superintendent and, contingent on the district, public question-and-answer sessions, or open school board meetings, which are broadcast on local cable television. The questions center around: "How would you keep the fine reputation we already have? What would you do if a parent disagreed with the consequence you gave to one of our students? What do you think is the role of parents in the school?"

The entire public school principal application process, from the time the credentials are submitted to the time a decision is made, can take up to three months. During this time, candidates' names are made public, sometimes causing embarrassment and loss of faith in the applicant's current job sphere.

With such a protracted time frame, it would seem there is sufficient time for a search committee to delve deeply into the candidates' personal qualities, as is done by human resource professionals in both independent schools and corporations. The middle manager hiring process is also lengthy in these settings.

I recently came across an independent school advertisement for an administrator akin to a public school principal. The ad read, "Looking

for someone who can guide and counsel middle school faculty in the resolution of interpersonal issues between or among faculty, students, parents, and others, and guide and monitor the professional development
of middle school faculty members . . . provide leadership in developing
and cultivating excellence in teaching and a dynamic curriculum. Please
submit five references, a letter of interest and a resume."

I phoned the independent school to find out about the hiring process
for this position and was informed of the procedure: There would be an
initial interview with the headmaster, followed by a full day of interviews
and observation of classes. Interviews would be conducted with department heads, with middle school and upper school teachers, and with the
dean of faculty. The applicant would eat lunch with students and teachers and would visit several classes in-between interviews. Then, the candidate would return for a third visit at which time he or she would teach
a class and would meet again with the headmaster. The whole process
would take about two months.

This hiring method, which is a month shorter than that of the public
school search, brings a broader range of candidates to a wider range of
settings. This process allows applicants greater opportunity to demonstrate interpersonal skills.

Turning now to the corporate world, given the recent corporate scandals, some companies are attempting to deflect future embarrassment
by trying to determine ahead of time whether their prospective managers have the interpersonal skills to do the job. These companies hire
a group of psychologists to interview and test managerial candidates.
Such interviews and tests are helpful in determining whether or not the
applicants have the interpersonal skills appropriate for building one-to-
one relationships with coworkers. Although it is costly to hire psychologists, corporations can refine candidate pools to reflect only those job
applicants who appear capable of promoting intraoffice relationships
and being successful in team work.

Since public school districts do not have enough money in their
budgets for hiring psychologists to test prospective school leaders,
they could create opportunities for teachers, union personnel, and
support staff to meet informally with their applicants, as independent
schools do. With a three-month hiring period, there is ample time between credential receipt and search committee formation for prospec-

tive principal candidates to meet with faculty. Teachers and support staff know who would be a good fit for their school. They know the culture of their school. We need to have the confidence in the professionalism of our teachers to determine which applicants are best suited to be their next principal.

SOME IMPLICATIONS FOR PRINCIPAL TRAINING PROGRAMS

Given our current culture of accountability and transparency, it seems more important now, than in the past, to determine the interpersonal skills of a prospective leader. Recently in Boston, for example, a prominent Catholic archbishop was forced to resign from office because he lost the trust of his faithful followers. Nationally, two prominent leaders removed themselves from a committee designed to investigate the terrorist attacks of September 11, 2001, and a Senate majority leader relinquished his post under increasing pressure from many Americans who were displeased with his formerly secret feelings about race. What this means is that leaders can no longer be out of touch with the sensibilities of their constituents. The public wants to know what is going on in government, religious institutions, schools, and corporations. To assuage the public, leaders need to develop trust in their constituents by reaching out and using the trust enhancers in this book.

The corporate scandals of Enron, WorldCom, Merrill Lynch, and so many other companies have caused people to pay attention to ethical leader behavior. There has been a certain greedy behavior among chief executive officers that is a reflection of a change in values. People no longer want corporate leaders to just make money, they want them to make it fairly and honestly.

For leaders of churches, synagogues, corporations, and schools, morale and teamwork play vital roles today. This is reflected in new business school courses on ethics, which emanate from courses of the 1940s. In 1947, for example, at Harvard Business School, a new required course appeared in the curriculum. The course was known as "Administrative Practices." This course taught students "how to get things done through people" (Callahan, 2002). "Ad Prac" (as it was known) promoted the management of human relations as an element of business leadership equally important to finance, production, and marketing. Business leaders have said that they found this course to be one of the most important they took at Harvard Business School.

How can schools of education capitalize on the same idea of "getting things done" through people? In education, we are working with people to impact young people, the next generation of corporate, religious, and school leaders. Why not prepare new principals to work collaboratively to "get things done" in the bureaucracies of public schooling? Schools of education could offer courses geared to human relations management. Based on my own experience, such courses are more valuable than courses on fiscal and plant management.

Now is the time to be inventive in our approach to principal education. With the projected national shortage of principals due to retirement, principal certification programs are springing up in nontraditional places. Nonprofit educational and professional organizations are teaming up with local universities and colleges to certify principals. Some of these organizations are sponsoring licensure programs in partnership with professional development groups and are being approved by state departments of education. Many of these new pathways to administrator licensure include weekend and summer study, expediting principal-training programs. Universities are offering doctoral degrees in education online. Some school systems are "growing their own principals" by teaming up with local colleges and offering on-site, after-school courses for prospective administrators.

Now is the time to listen to practitioners who are asking us to solicit their input, to keep their confidences, to resolve their conflicts, to share decision making, and to respect them personally and professionally. Now is the time for school leaders to be trained to work in diverse teams, to solve problems together, to brainstorm solutions, to gather data, take it apart, look at it, put it back together again, and reexamine it at a future date.

Now is the time for school leaders to be trained to listen actively and reach out to those teachers who want to contribute, but do not know how. Now is the time for school leaders to look at every member of a school as someone who touches the heart of every student who walks through that building day after day. Now is the time for every school leader to acknowledge the good work of teachers and support staff and to help, not threaten, those who want to do better, but do not have the skills. All of us are in this together. We are in education for the betterment of our students. We adults need to model for our students how we can build trusting relationships with one another.

6

CONCLUSION

Some of the ways of recruiting, retaining, and sustaining principals capable of promoting trusting relationships with their teaching staffs are: (1) restructuring the public school principal hiring process to determine relationship-building capabilities of aspiring principals; (2) modifying school leadership practices to encompass trust-enhancing behaviors enumerated in this book; and (3) revising principal-training programs to include people-management courses.

As we have seen in the preceding chapters, success as a school leader is based on trusting interpersonal relationships that are constructed and supported by the behaviors of the school leader. The specific behaviors are somewhat locally defined via communicative and supportive practices of the principal. These practices seem simple to effect, yet the hierarchical nature of the principal–teacher relationship and the focus on accountability make it more difficult to promote trust than could be imagined. The leader behaviors prescribed by principals and teachers in this book offer school leaders an opportunity for facilitating faculty trust.

The current focus on shared leadership and democratic governance in schools points to the need for principals and teachers to work together for the benefit of students. A relationship of trust is the foundation for such collaboration. At its heart, teaching is about building relationships, not only between teachers and students, but also between students and the world around them. The teaching-learning process is interactive, where teachers and students work together to create a community of learning.

For this kind of learning community to occur, principals and teachers need to model exemplary interaction. Principals can make or break schools through the policies, practices, and behaviors they develop around their teaching staffs. The importance of principal support is manifest in the high attrition rate of new teachers. New teachers list among their reasons for leaving the profession within five years of beginning their teaching a lack of administrative support in their school.

Now more than ever, principals and teachers are being held accountable for student achievement by state and federal legislation. Principals and teachers must collaborate to keep the high ranking of their schools. Collaboration requires faculty trust. This idea was echoed in the remarks of a K–12 educator, "Everyone is worried about how they are being judged. With increased pressure coming down from the state to increase test scores, I think we will see the relational trust (principal–teacher) problem grow" (*Institute for Educational Leadership [IEL] Connections,* 2003).

Just recently, the Institute for Educational Leadership (IEL) conducted an informal survey on trust in schools. Respondents unanimously agreed that trust was an essential component of effective school reform and/or leadership (*IEL Connections,* 2003). Many of the respondents claimed that trust was lacking in K–12 schools. They felt that the results of the lack of trust were the loss of creativity and innovation. This, of course, impacts school reform and student achievement. One of the IEL survey respondents, a college professor, summed it up by saying, "Reform will stagnate without trust, leadership will become coercion, and at best mediocrity will reign" (2003).

Educational policies fail to consider the needs and concerns of the teachers. Many of the current federal and state policies threaten teachers and principals by specifying sanctions if schools do not make what legislators call "adequate yearly progress." In this atmosphere, faculty trust is even more important, as teachers and principals need to work together to impact student achievement. Frustration can breed in schools where principals cannot build trusting relationships. This lack of unity between administrators and teachers filters down to students, undermining service to students and successful school improvement. Professional collaboration needs to be a common practice.

From my teacher conversations, it is clear that school leaders need to develop the people who deliver the service: teachers. That is the key to school improvement. We need to align school leadership in support of teachers by providing better communication and support between principals and teachers, thereby impacting the trust process.

Teachers and principals in the schools I visited were very interested in talking with me about trust. They felt this issue was extremely important to their work. As they described the process of what they thought it took to build trust within their schools, they wondered if a guide book existed, wherein they could find out how they were doing. These principals and teachers were looking for suggestions on how to improve their work relationships. They said they knew that the key to improving their own schools required that they get along well enough to focus their collective efforts on student achievement.

Effective school leaders need to balance their school agendas with building faculty trust and improving student achievement. Trust is almost a vicious circle, with the principal constantly trying to prove him- or herself by looking for situations to inspire faculty trust. The trust enhancers in this book are valuable to school leaders who want to keep trust in the forefront of their agenda.

Trust never feels entirely solid as it rests on the unstable foundation of individual teacher and principal perceptions of trust-building behaviors. Therefore, the more tangible these behaviors are, the more trust is apparent. When there is trust, it represents a positive bond between principal and teacher. This is important since there are few ways that principals have to make large bonds with their faculty given the nature of the evaluation system.

What really matters is that success in the impersonal, bureaucratic system of public schools as it is today is based on successful one-to-one interpersonal relationships constructed and supported by teachers and principals, relationships that are built on a foundation of interpersonal trust. The ultimate aim is to develop supportive relationships between teachers, administrators, students, and parents and to foster independence and growth for the children we teach.

7

AFTERWORD

Most of the suggested trust enhancers for principals evolved out of teacher and principal experiences within the contexts of their own school settings. These specific behaviors or practices are within human reach. What this means is that there are practical lessons here for any motivated individual who is willing to work in a focused, consistent manner.

The trust enhancers are not career-specific. When someone hears about being reliable, sharing decision making, or treating coworkers fairly, it seems obvious that these same principles would be helpful for any corporate executive, religious leader, politician, or physician.

Here, in summary, are those suggested trust enhancers, as I call them. There probably are more factors that engender trust—or barriers to trust—that need to be explored, but the following are the ones that teachers and principals mentioned again and again during my interviews with them.

SUPPORTIVE BEHAVIORS

Maintaining confidentiality. If a teacher wants to confide something in the principal, no matter what it is, and the confidence does not harm another person, the principal should keep the confidence. To gain the trust of the teacher, this confidence is crucial.

Treat all teachers fairly. This means that if one teacher has a personal problem and cannot, for example, fulfill a duty, the principal agrees to either do it or finds a substitute. Should a similar situation arise with another teacher, that teacher should be treated the same way.

Be consistently responsive. Each time the principal is called on to respond to a teacher, whether for a resource a teacher needs or a piece of information, the teacher waits for a response from the principal. If a teacher wants to know the status about a disciplinary matter, the principal needs to respond in a timely manner. If, for example, the computer teacher needs a new LCD monitor, the principal needs to get one for him or her, provided there is adequate funding in the school budget.

Demonstrate follow-through. Teachers expect their principal to do whatever he or she says he or she will do. If, for example, the principal offers to look into what other schools have done regarding initiating a new rubric system, then the principal needs to follow through and get the information back to the teachers.

Solicit input from teachers. Principals cannot be thoroughly knowledgeable about every discipline. Teachers are subject matter specialists. When, for example, a superintendent suggests to the principal that it is time to consider modifying the math curriculum, the principal should consult with the math teachers first.

Praise and recognize good work. Recognizing and respecting the people who are making positive contributions to the school, a focus on the positive, inspires interpersonal trust. There is a new approach called "appreciative inquiry" that is used to fix organizations that focus on the negative. I have always found that if a parent told me, as principal, how wonderful a particular teacher was, it was incumbent on me to inform the teacher about such praise. The teacher felt pleased and inspired with this positive feedback.

Be reliable. Teachers need to be able to count on their principal for anything. If there is a discipline issue, teachers need to know their principal will be there to support them. If there is a parent complaint, teachers need to know the principal will consult with them about it and act in the best interest of the student, contingent on teacher input.

Lead collegially. The principal can establish an administrative team as a school governance board. This team could be composed of representative teachers from the various disciplines, related arts, and special education. This team advises the principal and serves as a sounding board for the principal.

Respect teachers' opinions. When a teacher has an opinion about a new school policy, the teacher should be free to express how he or she feels about the policy and the principal should respect the teacher's opinion. If, for example, a parent complains that her youngster should be moved to a higher-level math class, the math teacher's opinion should be sought and valued.

Be considerate and caring about teachers' personal lives. In one of the schools I visited, the principal covered a class for a teacher who had to leave school because her child had been taken ill. The principal told me he did this whenever one of his teacher's had a family problem. When I was a principal, one of my teacher's father passed away and I covered her class so she could leave school to be with her family. Throughout the school year, that teacher repeatedly thanked me.

Be respectful of teachers' professionalism. Before implementing a new policy, practice, or curriculum, the principal should get some data from teachers on how the new practice would fit into the school environment. Teachers have a different perspective than the principal and often their perceptions serve to inform the principal of how something new would play out in the school setting.

Be willing to admit mistakes. Showing vulnerability is trust building. Teachers who see their principal as human, someone who makes mistakes, engenders compassion and respect along with trust. A principal who acknowledges his or her frequent typos in memos, for example, shows humility and endears him- or herself to the teachers.

COMMUNICATIVE BEHAVIORS

Confront conflict and try to resolve it. The principal needs to bring conflicts out in the open. If, for example, a group of teachers are disappointed with another group of teachers over the fact that the latter group is willing to do corridor duty for no additional stipend, it is up to the principal to confront each group separately, then together, and work out a compromise whereby everyone has been heard. Perhaps, a resolution might be worked out so that the principal seeks some volunteer parents to relieve some of the teachers from the extra duty or some teachers who are willing to do corridor duty may be relieved of a lunch duty.

Provide timely, accurate information. Teachers told me that one of the barriers to trust is misinformation and/or a lack of information. Misunderstandings across boundaries are common and when addressed build trust. Issues need to be dealt with as soon as they arise, in an open, honest manner. If a new central-office dictum is about to be implemented in a school, the principal needs to tell the teachers before they hear it from their colleagues. In that way, teachers will understand the rationale for the new mandate as well as have the information firsthand.

Articulate goals and expectations. It is important for the principal to be clear about what he or she expects from teachers. If, for example, test scores in math computation need to be a focus for the school year, the principal needs to discuss this with the teachers and they can, as a cohesive unit, collaborate to improve math test scores. Perhaps, the principal even needs to inform teachers that a certain percentage score should be attained by a specific percentage of students. Teachers then know what to strive for.

Practice empathic, active listening. It is difficult to listen to a teacher or group of teachers, especially for prolonged periods, when there are so many other things happening in a school each day. Yet, the principal needs to suspend all thoughts of what may have just happened on a school bus or what may happen in a meeting with the superintendent. The principal needs to focus on the teacher. If the principal can put him- or herself into the situation of that teacher and listen to what is being said, then the teacher will feel validated.

Be visible for informal dialogue. A principal who spends a lot of time in his or her office is not visible throughout the school. I heard about a principal who did not know many of the students in her small, elementary school because she spent so much time in her office. Teachers in that school complained that they had no one to go to when they had a problem. Parents found all this out at a local soccer game. They got together and confronted the principal about her inaccessibility, explaining that their children did not know her and that the teachers felt disconnected from their principal. It is important for the principal to be seen throughout the school building so that teachers can discuss whatever is on their minds.

Maintain open door policy/availability. Many teachers and principals I interviewed expressed the importance of being able to touch base whenever possible with their school leader. They said that principals should focus on teachers and students first and on paperwork second.

Plan meetings as necessary. Some teachers told me they had to attend too many meetings. Others told me there were not enough meetings with the principal. It is important to meet before a proposed agenda becomes so long that it is unwieldy.

Share decision making. Conferring with teachers about decisions offers the principal an opportunity to have a sounding board. By letting teachers hear various constraints of a given situation, teachers better understand the rationale behind the decision. The principal can convene the administrative team or the full faculty to discuss issues at hand.

LEADING FROM A BASIS OF FACULTY TRUST

Examples of the different trust enhancers actually come from practice. They serve as ways for practitioners to see how these trust enhancers play out in schools. When principals or other school leaders are new to their environments, much of the first year of their tenure is devoted to listening and observing in an effort to learn the culture of the school. I propose that the first year also be used to promote trust between principals and teachers. Principals need to spend a lot of face time in that first year, just getting to know the teachers and the staff, sharing stories, and looking for cultural similarities and differences.

Much of the first year of school leadership is spent becoming acclimated to routines and to personnel. A new principal needs to find out what is working well, what is valued, and what needs to be improved. For all of this to occur, the new school leader needs to become acquainted with the faculty, informing him- or herself about teachers' personal and professional lives. This means making phone calls to teachers in the evenings to find out how a new curriculum is being implemented, how team teaching is going, how a particular student is progressing, how a teacher's sick child is feeling, how professional development courses are going, and so on.

Doing all this takes time and the first year as a school leader in a new school is exhausting. But taking time to build relationships with the teaching staff is the most important thing a new principal can do. Trust rests on one-to-one principal–teacher relationships. Trust is the foundation for school improvement. In this age of accountability and school reform, it is well worth the principal's effort to reach out to teachers and forge trusting adult relationships.

REFERENCES

Archer, J. (2003). N.Y.C. Chancellor issues "report cards" on principals. *Education Week*, 22 (18), 4.

Ashby, D. E., and Krug, S. E. (1998). *Thinking through the Principalship.* Larchmont, NY: Eye on Education.

Barnes, K. M. (1994). *The organizational health of middle schools: Trust and decision making.* (Doctoral Dissertation, Rutgers, State University of New Jersey).

Barnes, L. B. (1981). Managing the paradox of organizational trust. *Harvard Business Review*, 107–116.

Barth, R. S. (1990). *Improving Schools from Within.* San Francisco: Jossey-Bass.

Bennis, W. G. (1994). *On Becoming a Leader.* Reading, MA: Perseus Books.

Blumberg, A., and Greenfield, W. (1980). *The Effective Principal: Perspectives on School Leadership.* Boston: Allyn and Bacon.

Blumberg, A., Greenfield, W. D., and Nason, D. (1978). The substance of trust between teachers and principals. *NASSP Bulletin*, 62 (9), 76–88.

Bogdan, R., and Biklen, S. (1998). *Qualitative Research in Education.* Boston: Allyn and Bacon.

Burns, J. M. (1978). *Leadership.* New York: Harper and Row.

Bushnell, D. (2002). Authors hail true leaders, old, young. *Boston Sunday Globe.* November 10, G1, G6.

Callahan, D. (2002). Making it. *Boston Sunday Globe.* December 8, D5.

Carnevale, D. G. (1988). *Organizational trust: A test of a model of its determinants.* (Doctoral Dissertation, Florida State University). Dissertation Abstracts International, volume 49–12A.

Chatfield, C. A. (1997). *The Trust Factor.* Santa Fe: Sunstone Press.

Checkley, K. (2000). Changing the way we think. *Education Update.* ASCD, 42 (8), 3.

Cho, A. (2002). Newton must restore trust in schools. *Boston Sunday Globe.* November 17, G5.

Cooper, R. K., and Sawaf, A. (1997). *Executive E.Q. Emotional Intelligence in Leadership and Organizations.* New York: Grosset/Putnam.

Copland, M. A. (2001). The myth of the superprincipal. *Phi Delta Kappan, 82* (7), 528–533.

Creswell, J. W. (1994). *Research Design: Qualitative and Quantitative Approaches.* Thousand Oaks, CA: Sage Publications.

Evans, K. M. (1992). *Trust and shared governance of schools: A qualitative approach.* Dissertation Abstracts International, A53/09, 3059.

Farmer, R. F., Gould, M. W., Herring, R. L., Linn, F. J., and Theobald, M. A. (1995). *The Middle School Principal.* Thousand Oaks, CA: Sage Publications.

Ferris, C. H. (1994). *A program for building trust between teachers and administrators to enhance the supervision/evaluation process.* Paper presented at AERA, New Orleans, April. (Eric Document Reproduction Service, Number 370 930).

Fullan, M. G. (1993). *What's Worth Fighting for in the Principalship.* Toronto: OPSTF.

Gibb, J. R. (1969). Dynamics of leadership. In F. D. Carver and T. J. Sergiovanni (Eds.). *Organizations and Human Behavior: Focus on Schools.* New York: McGraw-Hill.

Glesne, C. (1999). *Becoming Qualitative Researchers.* New York: Addison Wesley Longman.

Hausman, C. S., Crow, G. M., and Sperry, D. J. (2000). Portrait of the "ideal principal": Context and self. *NASSP Bulletin, 84* (617), 5–14.

Hernandez, A., and Mahoney, M. (2002). Is the private sector qualified to reform schools? *Education Week, 22* (3), 34, 38.

Hoerr, T. (2000). Doing things right or doing the right things? *Education Week,* 11 (35), 44, 47.

Hoffman, J. D. (1993). *The organizational climate of middle schools and dimensions of authenticity and trust.* (Doctoral Dissertation, Rutgers, State University of New Jersey).

Hoffman, J., Sabo, D., Bliss, J., and Hoy, W. K. (1994). Building a culture of trust. *Journal of School Leadership, 4,* 484–499.

Horton, T. R., and Reid, P. C. (1991). *Beyond the Trust Gap: Forging a New Partnership between Managers and Their Employers*. Homewood, IL: Business One Irwin.

Hoy, W. K., and Kupersmith, W. (1984). Principal authenticity and faculty trust: Key elements in organizational behavior. *Planning and Change*, 15, 80–88.

Hoy, W. K., and Kupersmith, W. (1985). The meaning and measure of faculty trust. *Educational and Psychological Research*, 5 (1), 1–10.

Hoy, W. K., and Tarter, C. J. (1988). The context of trust: Teachers and the principal. *The High School Journal*, 72 (1), 17–24.

Hoy, W. K., Tarter, C. J., and Kottkamp, R. B. (1991). *Open Schools/Healthy Schools: Measuring Organizational Climate*. Newbury Park, CA: Sage Publications.

Hoy, W. K., Tarter, C. J., and Witkoskie, L. (1992). Faculty trust in colleagues: Linking the principal with school effectiveness. *Journal of Research and Development in Education*, 26 (1), 38–45.

Institute for Educational Leadership Connections. (2002). Reader survey: Is trust the missing ingredient? 1 (2), November/December.

Institute for Educational Leadership Connections. (2003). TRUST (Commentary) 1 (3), January/February.

Keller, B. (1998). Principal matters. *Education Week*, 28 (11), 25–27.

King, S. D. (1996). *Trust and shared governance: A qualitative approach at the middle school level*. (Doctoral Dissertation, Marquette University).

Kotter, J. P. (1988). *The Leadership Factor*. New York: The Free Press.

Kotter, J. P. (1999). *On What Leaders Really Do*. Boston, MA: Harvard Business School Press.

Kottkamp, R., Mulhern, J., and Hoy, W. K. (1987). Secondary school climate: A Revision of the OCDQ. *Education Administration Quarterly*, 23, 31–48.

Kron, J. (1990). Effective middle level principal. In R. W. Hostrop. *The Effective School Administrator*. Palm Springs, CA: ETC Publications.

Kupersmith, W. (1983). *Leader behavior of principals and dimensions of teacher trust*. (Doctoral Dissertation, Rutgers, State University of New Jersey). Dissertation Abstracts International, 45, 365.

Lashway, L. (2000). Who's in charge? The accountability challenge. *Principal Leadership*. NASSP, 1 (3), 9–13.

Lewicki, R. J., and Bunker, B. B. (1996) Developing and maintaining trust in work relationships. In Kramer, R. M., and Tyler, T. R. *Trust in Organizations*. Thousand Oaks, CA: Sage Publications.

Likert, R. (1961). *New Patterns of Management*. New York: McGraw-Hill.

Likert, R. (1967). *The Human Organization: Its Management and Value*. New York: McGraw-Hill.

Mannion, P. T. (1998). *Trusting transformational principals: An empirical surprise.* Paper presented at AERA, San Diego, April. (Eric Document Reproduction Service, Number 420 926).

Maxwell, J. A. (1996). *Qualitative Research Design: An Interactive Approach.* Thousand Oaks, CA: Sage Publications.

McBride, M., and Skau, K. G. (1995). Trust, empowerment, and reflection: Essentials of supervision. *Journal of Curriculum and Supervision,* 10 (3), 262–277.

Merriam, S. B. (1988). *Case Study Research in Education: A Qualitative Approach.* San Francisco: Jossey-Bass.

Merriam, S. B. (1998). *Qualitative Research and Case Study Applications in Education.* San Francisco: Sage Publications.

Miles, M. B., and Huberman, A. M. (1994*). Qualitative Data Analysis: An Expanded Sourcebook* (2nd edition). Thousand Oaks, CA: Sage Publications.

Morgan, D. L. (1997). *Focus Groups As Qualitative Research.* Thousand Oaks, CA: Sage Publications.

Murphy, J. and Louis, K. S. (1994). *Reshaping the Principalship.* Thousand Oaks, CA: Corwin Press.

Nachmias, D. (1985). Determinants of trust within the federal bureaucracy. In D. H. Rosenbloom (Ed.). *Public personnel policy: The politics of civil service.* Port Washington, NY: Associated Faculty Press.

National Association of Elementary School Principals. (1997). *Proficiencies for Principals.* Alexandria, VA: NAESP.

Nori, J. (2000). The future of the middle level program. *Principal Leadership.* NASSP, 1 (2), 60–61.

Ouchi, W. G. (1981) *Theory Z.* Reading, MA: Addison-Wesley.

Owens, R. G. (1982). Methodological rigor in naturalistic inquiry: Some issues and answers. *Educational Administration Quarterly,* 18 (2), 1–21.

Palus, C. J., and Horth, D. M. (2002). *The Leader's Edge.* San Francisco: Jossey-Bass.

Pappano, L. (2001). The chalkboard. *Boston Sunday Globe.* May 13, L5–L6.

Preuss, P. G. (1980). *Content and process: A study of the relationship between the substance of trust and interpersonal relationships between teachers and principals.* (Doctoral Dissertation, Syracuse University). Dissertation Abstracts International, 41, 2390A.

Rooney, J. (2000). Survival skills for the new principal. *Educational Leadership,* 58 (1), 77–78.

Seitsinger, R. M., and Zera, D. A. (2002). Administrative systems and their responses to special education. *Educational Horizons,* 1 (81), 27–32.

Sergiovanni, T. J. (1990). *Value-Added Leadership.* Orlando, FL: Harcourt Brace Jovanivich.

Sergiovanni, T. J. (1996). *Leadership for the Schoolhouse.* San Francisco: Jossey Bass.

Sernak, K. (1998). *School Leadership—Balancing Power with Caring.* New York: Teachers College Press.

Tarter, C. J., Bliss, J. R., and Hoy, W. K. (1989). School characteristics and faculty trust in secondary schools. *Educational Administration Quarterly,* 25 (3), 294–308.

Tarter, C. J., Sabo, D., and Hoy, W. K. (1995). Middle school climate, faculty trust and effectiveness: A path analysis. *Journal of Research and Development in Education,* 29 (1), 41–49.

Villani, S. (1999). *Are You Sure You're the Principal? On Being an Authentic Leader.* Thousand Oaks, CA: Corwin Press.

Wolcott. H. F. (1990). *Writing up Qualitative Research.* Newbury Park, CA: Sage Publications.

Wolfe, A. (2002). The men who disappeared. *Boston Sunday Globe.* December 22, D1.

Yin, R. K. (1994). *Case Study Research: Design and Methods* (2nd edition). Thousand Oaks, CA: Sage Publications.

INDEX

admitting mistakes/vulnerability, 15–16, 28, 35, 38, 41, 44, 52, 54, 69

advertisements for principals, 56, 57–58

advisory groups, 5–7

appreciative inquiry, 68

Archer, J., 54–55

attitude of principal, 12, 23, 34–35, 41, 51–52, 53

authenticity, 11, 12, 15–16, 22–23, 34, 43, 45, 46

autonomy, 46, 53

availability, 15, 38, 39, 41, 49, 51, 70–71

barriers to trust, 1–3, 38, 70; miscommunication, 25–26, 28

beliefs, 23, 24, 44, 46

budget control, 55

business leaders, 59–60

caring behavior, 36, 42, 52, 69

certification of principals, 60

collaboration, 63–64

collegiality, 17, 30, 35, 36–38, 49, 50–51, 54, 69

communication, 16, 17, 21, 23, 32, 45, 54, 69–71; accuracy, 26–27; electronic, 26–27, 29–30, 51; face-to-face conversation, 27, 30; informal dialogue, 16, 21, 28, 34, 44, 47, 49, 50, 51, 70–71; interpretations, 25–26; leader behaviors, 25–33; one-to-one interviews, 16, 17, 23, 27, 51; principal's perspective, 21, 25–27, 28–30, 31–32; teacher's perspective, 22, 28, 30–31, 32–33

confidence, 17–18, 23, 33, 44

ABOUT THE AUTHOR

Dr. Phyllis A. Gimbel has enjoyed a diverse career in education. She has worked in independent, suburban, and urban settings as a French and Spanish teacher, department chair, middle school principal and consultant, and superintendent intern. She spent her junior year of college in Paris, France, and Santander, Spain, studying at both the Sorbonne and the Universidad Menendez Pelayo. She earned a B.A. in French and Spanish from Hood College, Frederick, Maryland, and later received an M.A. in French from Columbia University in New York. After her children were grown, she returned to graduate school and earned a master's in education in 1995 from the Harvard University Graduate School of Education. In 2001, she received her doctorate in education, specializing in leadership in schooling, from the University of Massachusetts–Lowell's Graduate School of Education. Dr. Gimbel currently serves as the coordinator of Project Open, a university and public school collaborative with Boston College, Boston University, Brandeis University, Lesley University, and Watertown, Massachusetts, public schools.